Design Your Own Destiny

See what people are saying about
Design Your Own Destiny

"Mary's process is practical and effective. It is sure to help anyone facing major life choices."

—Stedman Graham, author of *You Can Make It Happen*
and *Identity: Your Passport to Success*

"Mary Molloy has a **powerful message** and a **concrete process** to share with the world. Her message is that we can all live the life of our dreams—it's up to us. It's a matter of opening up our minds and hearts to the possibilities presented to us from the Universe. **Mary's life planning process has helped many, many people get from where they are to where they dream of being. Her book is a powerful contribution to humanity that could change your life!**"

—Marc Allen, author of *Visionary Business, The Millionaire Course*
and publisher of New World Library

"Mary Molloy's Life Planning methodology offers us a **smart and innovative approach to personal development**. Her uncanny ability to easily apply and adapt business skills to help people personally achieve what they never thought they could is nothing short of brilliant. After completing it for yourself, you will find you, too, will want to share your successes and this remarkable method with others in your life. It really works!"

—Laura T. Rivela, L.C.S.W.-R, B.C.D., division director,
Behavioral Health Programs, Family Service League, Inc.

"We are entering a new age, a time on earth when it is easier than ever to wake up and realize the obvious. Intuitively we grasp that we are out of balance and that the best thing we can do for the world, our loved ones and our own happiness is to be the very best self we can be. Our world is going to become a better place one person at a time and Mary Molloy has discovered the many practical secrets that allow you to have your destined best "self actualized" life in this world. **I am enthusiastically recommending this book to family, friends and patients.**"

—William Evans, MD, psychiatrist

"True balance is achieved when we strive to meet the needs of others, and fulfill our own aspirations in the process. *Design Your Own Destiny* **focuses on the balance in life and how to attain and sustain it.**"

—Gia Milo-Slagle, product manager, McKesson Corporation

"I have worked with Mary Molloy personally and professionally. Her **methods and tools are concrete, practical, easy to use and understand and have helped so many people to live the life of their dreams** by opening up their minds, hearts and spirits to the possibilities being presented to them. Readers who follow the process of this book have a real chance to achieve success. I highly recommend *Design Your Own Destiny* to people who are motivated to explore their current life situations and use this book to design their own destinies."

—Susan Kimper, MSN, RN-BC nursing director

"Mary Molloy has made an outstanding contribution to everyone's personal development. She has created **a process for simplifying the complexity in life's choices**. As an executive coach, I am recommending this book to all of my clients and friends—it's guaranteed to make your life's choices conscious and intentional."

—Deborah Slobodnik, principal, Options for Change, LLC

"*Design Your Own Destiny* goes beyond the typical, "Vision, what you want and PRESTO, it is manifest." Rather, Mary takes the reader on a journey of self-discovery partnered with practical application. With a life well planned, Mary had no idea what was in store when her husband of over 25 years passed away from esophageal cancer. Working through her loss and devastation, Mary took her message to a soul level. *Design Your Own Destiny* combines practical, keep your feet on the ground strategies with a high spiritual flavor. Join Mary on your own journey of self-discovery and awakening as you Design Your Own Destiny.

—Kathleen Gage, business owner, inspirational speaker, best-selling author and creator of The Street Smarts Marketing System

Design Your Own Destiny

LIFE PLANNING FOR THE 21ST CENTURY

Mary A. Molloy

© 2012 Mary A. Molloy

ISBN: 978-0-9853796-7-4
LCCN: 2012935757

Printed in the U.S.A.

Book cover and interior design by Anita Jones, Another Jones Graphics

Front book jacket photo by Jimbo Marshall of Hell Yeah Studios
http://www.hellyeahstudios.com
and Mahijeet Singh & the CS Soft Solutions Team
http://www.cssoftsolutions.com

Back book jacket photo by Liz McNeill Jenkins,
http://www.lizmjenkinsphotography.com.
Facebook Liz McNeill Jenkins Photography

"Man in circle" drawings by Stephen Hodecker

Ballerina photo by Amy Wilton, Amy Wilton Photography, Camden, ME,
www.amywiltonphotography.com.

Also available by Mary A. Molloy:
The Buck Starts Here—Profit Based Sales and Marketing Made Easy
(co-authored with Michael K. Molloy)

About this book

I would like to thank you for your interest in *Design Your Own Destiny —
Life Planning for the 21st Century*. This life planning methodology and its
business planning counterpart have helped thousands of people from all
walks of life and every economic level to create plans that have changed
their lives and have fulfilled their dreams.

There are two key premises in this life planning approach. The first
is that everyone's life is most happy and fruitful when he or she is in balance; and the second is that a life plan must consider the person's whole
being—not just bits and pieces of it. It must take into account the person's
mental and physical world, but also it must consider their emotional and
spiritual one as well. What this means to you is that the plan needs to
incorporate who you are, what talents you have, what your dreams are,
and ultimately where you want to go in the short and long term. It must
provide the tools to help you determine which life choices are best for
you based on your own personal values.

After speaking with other life coaches and counseling professionals,
I have found that these two premises differentiate this strategy from anything currently available. There is nothing like it.

This unique life planning process begins with balance—the determination of whether you are "in balance" or "out of balance." From there, we
create a life plan that focuses on your "whole" being—your mind, your
physical/material world (your health and wealth), your relationship to
something higher than you (God/the Universe) and your emotions.

By focusing on these key components, we can create a powerful life
plan to help you fulfill your goals and dreams.

Design Your Own Destiny provides you with a step-by-step, easy-
to-learn process that you can use to create your own life plan. It brings
you from where you are now to where you want to go. In this book, I
teach you not only how to create the plan for the life of your dreams, but
also how to measure the plan and adjust it to your real life as day-to-day
events and circumstances unfold.

From my work with thousands of people worldwide from all walks of life I know that this methodology works. This powerful and effective tool can change your life—as it has for many others. I am excited about offering you this opportunity to Design Your Own Destiny!

Mary A. Molloy

This Book is Dedicated to:

Mary Gagliardo

for being such a great mother, inspiration and blessing

Michael Molloy

for being my twin flame and my first true love

Paul Brown

for being my best friend and beloved husband

Contents

DESIGN YOUR OWN DESTINY

Foreword

Success comes to those who are conscious.
Most of us live our lives unconsciously.

—NAPOLEON HILL

This book has taken many years and many changes in my life to write. I began to write this book in 2003. At that point I had been married to an extremely wonderful man named Michael Kevin Molloy for twenty-five years. Michael and I were not only husband and wife; we were best friends and business partners. In 1990, we established an internationally known management consulting firm, TRB Consulting Group, which specializes in sales, marketing and business planning. Through the years, Michael and I worked with over 16,000 people in 39 countries (I personally worked with over 11,000 people). Our clients included Hewlett Packard, Microsoft, Motorola, Siemens Healthcare and hundreds of small- to medium- sized companies worldwide.

In the course of our work together, Michael and I co-authored a business bestseller called *The Buck Starts Here—Profit Based Sales and Marketing Made Easy*. We won the Clarion Award for the best nonfiction book of the year. I also authored a new book entitled *The Partnering Ten Commandments—Partner for Profit*, which is in the process of being published.

In 2003, I was asked to speak to a group of women in Manchester, NH. In preparing for this meeting, I decided that I needed to provide them with a tool that could help them get from "here" to "there" (wherever here and there were for them). As I began to design this tool, I realized that it is important to look at the whole person in creating a life planning strategy. I didn't want to put together just a list of "to do's" nor did I want to put together a process that dealt only with jobs and career. I wanted to design something that focuses on a person as a whole—one that allows for the comingling of the spirit of the person with something higher than themselves.

I have been an avid reader and student of empowerment, spirituality and metaphysics for many years and have thoroughly enjoyed reading, studying and assimilating works from Ernest Holmes, *A Course in Miracles*, Gary Renard, Marc Allen, James Allen, Napoleon Hill, David Hawkins, Esther and Jerry Hicks, Eckhart Tolle and many, many others. As I created this methodology, I decided to incorporate the idea of balance within oneself (with one's mind, with one's physical world, with one's emotions) with one's balance with God or the Universe. Once balance is determined, then we can build a plan focusing on the core values, talents, joys in life and dreams of people as well as their missions in life. Because life is so filled with choices, I designed assessment tools that help people to determine the best options for them.

Since the time of the inception of this life planning methodology, I have worked with hundreds of people worldwide to create their life plans. I have done life plans for people of all ages, genders and cultures—for people from all walks of life—business people, artists, doctors, lawyers, nurses, housewives, musicians, masseuses and beauty pageant queens! In addition to helping individuals, these plans can be beneficial to couples. In a relationship, it's important that both people are on the same page with their life plans.

In 2006, my life went through a huge loss when my husband Michael died of esophageal cancer. During that time, I put the book down and could not write it. I was devastated and really didn't want to go on with my own life, but I realized that I had to. I had a mission that I had to pursue. There really was no choice. I had to rebuild my life and start again. I began with my own dreams, what I wanted for myself. I applied the concepts and principles that you see in this book to my own life—as I continue to do to this day, every day.

When my husband died, I realized that I was totally out of balance and that I needed to focus on things that would bring me back into balance. Michael was such a huge presence in my life and the loss of him put a huge "hole" in the middle of my very being.

Over time, I began to slowly heal. I met and married a wonderful man, a psychiatrist, Dr. Paul Brown. Paul encouraged me to refocus on my life planning methodology and continue to write this book, the very work that you have here before you.

This book is my gift to you. My goal is to help you to get what you want out of your life. Everyone has talents and one of mine enables me to take complex subjects and explain them in such a way as to make them easy. I do this by creating processes where I break the subject down into bite size pieces so that the content becomes easy to understand. All of my methodologies consist of strategies, tools and techniques that are comprehensive, easy to use and work in a step-by-step manner. This book can give you the answers to a subject that is near and dear to your heart, which is: *How do I know what I want from my own life and how can I create it?*

Please note that in the creation of this book I sometimes combined two or three people's life plans as examples. By doing this I was able to better able to teach the content and demonstrate it to you—my readers.

I hope that you enjoy my book and that you use it to bring more balance and joy into your own life. I also hope it helps you to achieve the life of your dreams. Please write to me at mary@maryamolloy.com and tell me how my book and life planning process have helped you. I welcome all comments and feedback. If you get stuck or need a private life plan or coaching, I've included my contact information so you don't have to go through this alone.

Introduction

Destiny is no matter of chance.
It's a matter of choice.

—William Jennings Bryan

Are we at the whim of destiny or can we choose and Design Our Own Destiny?

Have you ever thought about the word "destiny"? According to Wikipedia, which is an online dictionary, destiny is defined as a "predetermined course of events. It may be conceived as a predetermined future, whether in general or of an individual. Destiny is seen as a sequence of events that is inevitable and unchangeable."

Let's go with this definition. What this basically says is that we cannot change what we are destined to become. So, here's my question to you: How do we *know* what we're "destined" to become? How do we *know* what is in store for us—or what the end result of our lives is supposed to be? If we're destined by some agency outside of our conscious selves—say God or the Universe—how many of us have been told what we're destined to do or become?

Let's take the idea a step further. Could it be that when we act upon our dreams and take action that the end result of our actions *is* our destiny? Could it be that part of our journey in this lifetime is to discover how to act upon our dreams and make them come true? Could it be that ultimately our destiny is the end result of those actions, a time when some of us act upon our dreams and others do not?

We are each so different, but almost all of us have dreams that we wish would come true. Many just wish and wish. Others wish and then act—sometimes haphazardly, sometimes purposefully. Others wish that they knew *how* to make their dreams come true.

This is what this book is all about. It's about designing your own destiny. It's about giving you a tool to help you get from here to there—

wherever "there" is for you. *Design Your Own Destiny* provides a framework, a methodology that can help you to design a life plan to make your dreams come true.

What is a life planning process?

All of us have heard of business plans. Corporations do them all of the time and the phrase is very common. Some of us have heard of life plans, but in my experience, most of the life plans that I have seen are really based around careers, work and jobs. People's talents (what they are good at) are taken into account and these talents are then matched with potential careers. This is helpful to a certain extent but it really doesn't take into account the *whole* person. There is so much more to each of us than our talents and our careers, work or jobs.

The difference in this life planning strategy from many others currently available is that this process looks at you as a whole person. It looks at: who you are; what is important to you; what your talents, joys and dreams are; and how you can achieve your dreams. This book is complete. It teaches you what is important from a life planning perspective. In an easy to understand format, it provides examples from other people's life plans on how they used the strategies and tools to create the life of their dreams.

How does this life planning process work?

Each life is complex. We all have so many aspects to our personalities, our needs, our wants, our visions and our dreams. Because we are each so unique, I created this process to help you to focus not only on what is important to you but how you can get what you want out of your own life. This book covers the following topics:

- **Chapter 1: Are You In Balance?**
  This chapter provides an excellent tool to help you assess your own balance—whether you are "in balance" or "out of balance." If you are out of balance, you can use the ideas and strategies in this book to help you get back into balance. Once you achieve balance, we can accelerate into your life plan.

- **Chapter 2: Let's Talk About You—Your Core Values, Your Talents and Your Joys in Life**
  This chapter provides you with a process to look at your own core values and look at your talents and joys in life. Sometimes

people have talents that give them no joy. Others have talents they don't use. Your core values, your talents and your joys should match up with each other. In this chapter, we use a process that allows you to line up all of the things that are important to you.

- **Chapter 3: Your 'Self Talk' and the Power of Belief**
  In this chapter we explore what you say about yourself—to yourself—in the quiet confines of your mind and how it makes a difference in your life experiences. We talk about the impact of your beliefs. And, lastly, we focus on your mission in life. Why are you here on this earth right now? This chapter provides you with the tools to examine all of these concepts for yourself and helps you to determine whether you are on the right track with your "self talk" and your beliefs.

- **Chapter 4: Your Dreams**
  This chapter examines dreaming and the power of commitment in making your own dreams come true. By drawing your dreams you allow your subconscious mind to play with the possibilities. Other people's dreams are included with discussions on how they made their dreams come true.

- **Chapter 5: Evaluate Your Alternatives**
  This chapter provides a great way to assess the choices in your life. It offers a way to determine which choice is the best for you through the use of Ben Franklin "T" charts and a Life Choices Assessment tool. Once you learn how to use these tools, choosing the best option for you in most life circumstances not only will be possible, it will be easy! With creativity, this tool can be applied to the many choices that you may be facing in your life.

- **Chapter 6: Create a Life Choice Map**
  Once you determine what you want, how will you get there from here? A map, of course! We've always heard that a picture is worth a thousand words. Okay, what does your map/your picture look like? This chapter provides an excellent tool to map out how you will get from where you are now to where you want to go. It focuses not only on the actions that need to be taken, but also on the people, the resources you need and how long it will take for you to get there from here.

- **Chapter 7: Measure and Adjust Your Life Plan**
  In this chapter, we discuss easy ways to measure your life plan to see whether you're on track. If you're not, this chapter discusses how to adjust your plan to optimize the results. If your plan is taking too long, strategies and ideas are discussed to help you speed it up.

- **Chapter 8: Harmonic Alignment—Closing the Loop with Balance**
  As we began this book in a state of balance, we end with various approaches and strategies to counter balance—focusing on how to maintain ongoing balance and harmony in our lives.

So now let's begin with your life plan!

CHAPTER ONE

Are You In Balance?

People with great gifts are easy to find,
but symmetrical and balanced ones never.

—Ralph Waldo Emerson

Did you ever notice that some of the happiest people in life are also the most balanced people? These are the people who look at life realistically yet optimistically. They try to keep balance in their energy levels, their thoughts, their activities and in their lives. They look at life as a whole. This is something that needs to be focused on by everyone. The more *in balance* we are, the happier we are and the better we can deal effectively with the difficult situations that life may present to us.

As life situations occur, we may decide we want to change our lives—maybe move on to the next step or stage in life. Therefore, it is very helpful to determine how in balance we are every so often. Perhaps this is where you are now. You might be looking at getting out of or changing a current situation, or by contrast, you might be looking at all of the fun things that you would like to do. Before you start planning for the next step in your life, take a few minutes to assess yourself and your balance. How in balance are you?

Take a look at Figure 1.1. There are four points in every life that need to be in balance. They are your mind **(Intellectual)**; your material world, meaning your body's health and your wealth **(Physical)**; your relation-ship to God or the Universe **(Spiritual)**; and your feelings **(Emotional)**. These four focal points are the main contributors to health, happiness, peace of mind, security, prosperity and balance.

Figure 1.1

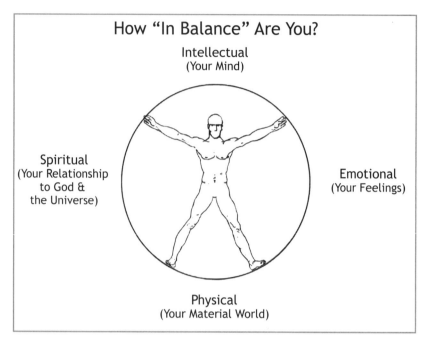

I call the center of the human in Figure 1.1 (his navel) his balance point. Have you ever heard anyone asking you to give an opinion based on gut feeling? We have all been given a built-in radar detector at birth by God or the Universe, and that radar detector is our *gut feeling*. You will find that when you use your gut feeling to answer a question or to determine how you feel about something, the answer that comes from your gut is usually the right answer. This part of your body is your balance point.

The importance of your gut

Many of us prefer to live our lives thinking and making decisions with our heads or by our hearts. Physically and physiologically, our brains tend to be dominant in either the left lobe or the right lobe. People who depend largely on the left side of their brains tend to make decisions by analysis. These people are called "left-brain" thinkers, and they are very common in developed countries. This is mostly how we're taught in school. Left-brain thinkers experience a situation, then they analyze it. They judge/interpret it; then they act based on what their *head* tells them to do.

People who have the dominant lobe on the right side of their brains tend to make decisions based on their feelings or emotions. These people are called "right-brain" thinkers. Many right-brain thinkers tend to be more artistic. Right-brain thinkers experience a situation and then they feel certain emotions about what they just experienced. This feeling leads them to take action based on what their *heart* tells them.

Some people are actually equally lobed. Their brains experience about the same amount of activity on both sides. These people move quickly between their right and left brains when making a decision. It is easier for them to base decisions on analysis and feelings at the same time. It is also easier for them to jump back and forth between looking at a spreadsheet and looking at a picture.

No matter what your thinking style is, you need both your head and your heart to come to a balanced decision. Your head and your heart come together in your gut as your gut feeling. As human beings, we have been given a built-in barometer. It is where our minds or intellect intersects with our heart or emotions. What your gut tells you is what you *really* think and what you *really* feel. In all aspects of our lives, the best place to look for answers is in the gut—inside you, at your core. It's important that we recognize the value and importance of our gut and our gut feelings. Most of the time, when we ignore our gut feelings, we get into trouble. So be aware and listen to the voice that comes from deep down inside you.

> *Be aware of wonder. Live a balanced life—learn some and think some and draw and paint and sing and dance and play and work every day some.*
>
> —ROBERT FULGHUM

> *Your head and your heart come together in your gut!*
> What your gut tells you is what you *really* think
> and what you *really* feel.

Step One: Assess your mind (your intellect)

Let's begin to determine your level of balance. Let's start with your mind. Are you in balance or are you out of balance intellectually? Do you need to use your mind more? Do you need to learn new things? Are you using your mind enough? Or conversely, do you need to use your mind less? Is your mind too active—so active that it needs to be calmed down?

Figure 1.2

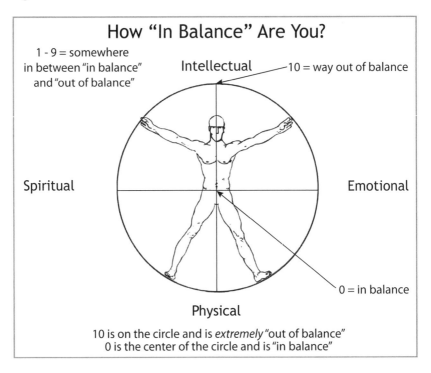

If you look at Figure 1.2, we call *balance* the center of the body. If you are *in balance* in a particular area, rate yourself a zero (0). If you are *way out of balance*, then rate yourself '10'. If you are *somewhat out of balance*—somewhere in between, not quite in balance but not totally out of balance—then rate yourself somewhere between '1' and '9'. Realize that you are using a *gut feeling* here to determine your own level of balance. That is okay. Your gut feeling is right, so trust it. Go with whatever number you tell yourself is correct. It is best to use whole numbers, not decimals, when scoring yourself.

In order to assess yourself, get out a piece of paper and on the top write the words, "My Balance Scorecard." Use Figure 1.3 as a guide and draw a circle with vertical and horizontal lines through it and place the words, "Intellectual," "Physical," "Health," "Wealth," "Spiritual" and "Emotional" on it. Also use Figure 1.3 as an example and give yourself a score for your Intellectual balance on your personal balance scorecard. You can also graph your score if you so desire. To assist you in graphing, refer to Figures 1.3, 1.6, 1.7 and 1.8.

Question One: Are you in balance or out of balance intellectually? What score do you give yourself?

In Figure 1.3 John rated himself a '5' in Intellectual. He feels that he needs to learn more and is somewhat out of balance intellectually. Although John uses his mind in his job, he feels that he is constantly in "think mode." It's almost as if he has to soothe or calm his mind. John also has gaps in his learning. He feels that if he finishes his degree, he will get a better job over time.

Figure 1.3

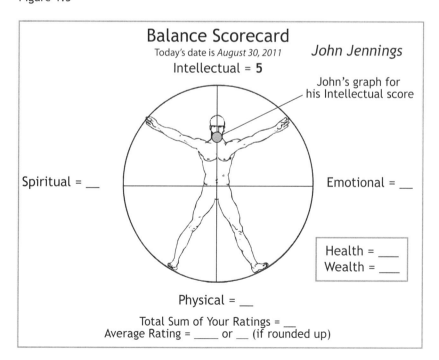

Balance Scorecard
Today's date is *August 30, 2011*   *John Jennings*
Intellectual = **5**

John's graph for his Intellectual score

Spiritual = __

Emotional = __

Health = ___
Wealth = ___

Physical = __

Total Sum of Your Ratings = __
Average Rating = ____ or __ (if rounded up)

Step Two: Assess your body, your material world and your physical wellbeing

When you think of the balance of the physical aspect of you, as in all of the balance factors, this is a subjective judgment. It is your opinion of your situation and how okay you are with it. I've done life plans for homeless people. In one life plan, I asked a woman (let's call her Susan) how she would rate her physical situation. This woman was extremely overweight and she was homeless. Yet she rated herself "in balance" for the physical aspect of her life. She said that she was okay with her current physical situation but that she wanted to make many changes to her life which included getting an education and getting an apartment so that she was no longer homeless. This being said, if your physical situation is not acceptable by other people's standards, but you are okay with it and you feel that you are in balance, then you *are* in balance.

Whatever *you* say about yourself is true for you.

Now ask yourself if you are in balance or out of balance physically. Think of "Physical" as the material aspect of your life. So, in this context, the physical aspect of you would include both your health (your body) and your wealth (your money, your material world and your physical surroundings). Did you ever hear of the term *fiscal* in relation to money in business? When companies start the beginning of a financial year, they begin their fiscal year. So let's use the word *fiscal* in the context of your life as well as your money—your financial "health"—and let's look at it as a component of your physical balance.

Your body—Your health

Let's start with your body and your health. Is your physical body in balance? Do you need to exercise more? Do you have a physical condition of some sort that puts you out of balance? If you are in balance, give yourself a '0' in Health. If you are *way out* of balance, give yourself a '10'. If you are somewhere in between, rate yourself between '1' and '9'. Go with your gut feeling. Use Figure 1.4 as an example as you ask yourself how in balance you are in your own body. Place your answer on your personal balance scorecard.

Question Two—Part One: Are you in balance or out of balance in your body / your health? What score do you give yourself?

In Figure 1.4 John rated himself a '2' in Health. He is pretty much in shape but he is not totally satisfied with the health of his body. He feels that he needs to exercise more and to eat healthier. John feels that these changes are vital to help him calm his mind.

Figure 1.4

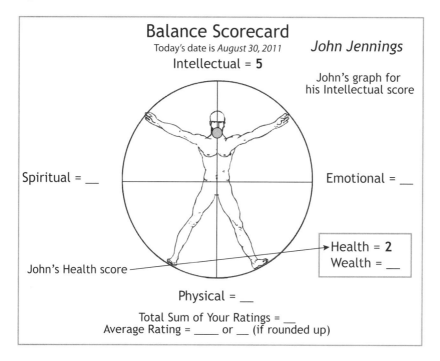

Balance Scorecard
Today's date is *August 30, 2011*   *John Jennings*
Intellectual = **5**

John's graph for his Intellectual score

Spiritual = __

Emotional = __

▸Health = **2**
Wealth = __

John's Health score

Physical = __

Total Sum of Your Ratings = __
Average Rating = ____ or __ (if rounded up)

Your wealth—Your material world

Now let's assess your material world. Include your surroundings, the things that you own and your satisfaction with this, your possessions and your financial situation (your wealth) in this assessment. Are you in balance or out of balance in your Wealth category? This is your judgment of your perception of your balance level in this area of your life. If you are in balance, give yourself a '0' in Wealth. If you are way out of balance, give yourself a '10'. If you are somewhere in between, rate yourself between '1' and '9'. Give yourself a score, place it on your personal balance scorecard and graph it as shown. Use Figure 1.5 as an example.

> *Question Two—Part Two: Are you in balance or*
> *out of balance in your wealth—in your material world?*
> *What score do you give yourself?*

In Figure 1.5 John gave himself a '4' in Wealth. He is not making as much money as he wants and he feels that he is out of balance in this area of his life. Things are not working smoothly for him financially and he sometimes feels out of control with his finances. John's financial situation is by no means dire because John has a job which allows him to pay his bills and provide for his family. However, money gets very tight on occasion and John needs to bring in more money over time.

Figure 1.5

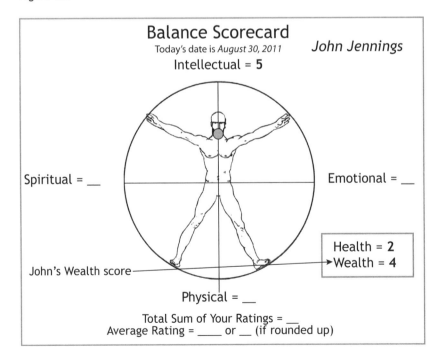

Balance Scorecard
Today's date is *August 30, 2011*   *John Jennings*
Intellectual = **5**

Spiritual = __

Emotional = __

Health = 2
→Wealth = 4

John's Wealth score

Physical = __

Total Sum of Your Ratings = __
Average Rating = _____ or __ (if rounded up)

Finally, ask yourself how in balance your *entire* Physical situation is. Consider your body, your finances, your surroundings: your entire material world. Sometimes people average the scores that they give themselves for Health and for Wealth. Other times they skew the scores in favor of one or the other. It's up to you. Again, this is subjective and whatever you say in your gut about yourself is what you believe—so let's go with it. Give yourself an overall Physical score somewhere between '0' and '10' (0 being in balance; 10 being totally out of balance) on your personal balance scorecard. Place a mark on the graph on your personal balance scorecard. Use the example in Figure 1.6 to assist you.

> *Question Two—Part Three: Are you in balance or*
> *out of balance in the overall physical aspect of your life?*
> *What overall score do you give yourself?*

In Figure 1.6, John assessed his overall Physical score as a '4'. The average between John's Health score of '2' and John's Wealth score of '4' is '3'. However, John rated himself as '4' in the overall Physical aspect of his life. He said that he felt that a '4' is more correct with what is going on with his Physical world. He felt that his money problems skew his whole physical situation and that his gut tells him that he's a '4' not a '3' in the Physical aspect of his life. John is right about his score because this is his perception. Please note that whatever score a person gives themselves is true for them!

Figure 1.6

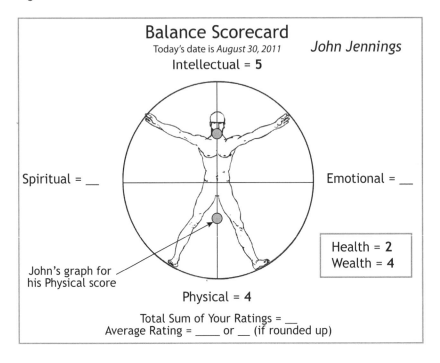

Step Three: Assess your relationship with God or the Universe—
something bigger than you

Question: Do you believe in a Higher Power—someone or something bigger than you? You can call this being God, Jesus, Buddha, Allah, Krishna, Goddess, Confucius, Spirit Being, Holy Spirit, Spiritual Mind, Creator, anything. Do you believe in a power higher than you? Sometimes people ask me, "Are you talking about religion here? Are you asking me if I believe in religion?" No! I am definitely not talking about religion here. I'm talking about your relationship with God or a Higher Power. I'm talking about your spirituality and your spiritual balance. Are you in balance with God?

If you don't believe in God, that's okay. Do you believe that the Universe is bigger than you are and that the Universe has power? Do you believe in any sort of a Higher Power? If so, are you in balance with this Higher Power?

Someone asked me recently, "What if I don't believe in God at all? I'm an atheist. Does that mean that I'm not in balance on my Spiritual score?" I responded, "Are you okay with this aspect of who you are? Are you okay with not believing in any deity or Higher Power whatsoever? Are you in balance with this side of yourself?" His response was, "Yes, I'm okay and I'm in balance." So, then, it is okay and he is in balance. Remember, balance is what you say it is. If you say that you are in balance in a certain aspect of your life and you really believe that this is true, then you are in balance!

Now, rate yourself on the Spiritual aspect of you according to the scale that we've outlined already. '0' is in balance, '10' is way out of balance, and '1 - 9' is somewhere in between. Where do you stand? Place a score on your personal balance scorecard and graph the number using Figure 1.7 as an example to follow.

Question Three: Are you in balance or out of balance spiritually? What score do you give yourself?

In Figure 1.7 John rated himself as '4' in Spiritual. He does believe in God and he feels somewhat out of balance with this aspect of his life. For a long time now John has felt that something is missing in his life. He belonged to an organized church as a child but he began to fall away from the tenets of this church when he was a teenager. John and his wife decided recently that they would look for a local church to join, but they feel that this church needs to coincide with their beliefs about life, God and spirituality.

On an even bigger scale, John has begun to question his life's purpose—why he is here in this world. He feels that he needs to explore this further and decide what the right path is for him. He feels that he needs to make some major changes in his life but he first needs to think about why he is here before he makes radical changes that will affect his life and his family's lives. Whatever he chooses to do, he will not do it in a vacuum but he will do it by involving his wife and his children.

Figure 1.7

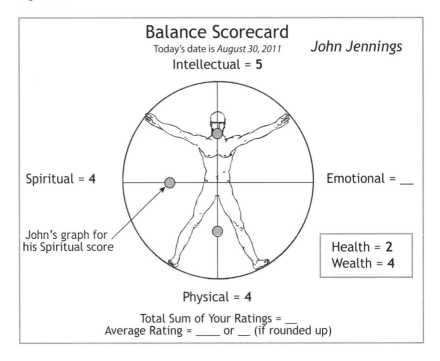

Step Four: Assess your emotional wellbeing

Where are you emotionally? Are you in balance or out of balance? Do you handle everyday life difficulties with an uncomfortable level of emotion or are you able to ride them out fairly evenly? Do you blame others for where you are in your life? Do you take things too personally?

Even though you might be facing a difficult time in life, you still might be in balance emotionally. Emotions tend to change. On bad days, we might feel emotional and out of control. On good days, we might feel more in balance. Let's focus on where you are right this minute. Are you in balance or out of balance emotionally? If you feel in balance, then rate yourself a '0'. If you feel out of balance emotionally, rate yourself somewhere between a '1' and a '10'. As before graph the score that you gave yourself. Use Figure 1.8 to help you with the graphing.

Keep in mind that life does not always go the way we want. The question is how you deal with the situations that you face. You might not like them and would like to change them. That's okay. This is why you are creating a life plan now and it is what we are going to look at in later chapters. Right now though, rate your Emotional balance.

Question Four: Are you in balance or out of balance
emotionally? What score do you give yourself?

In Figure 1.8 John gave himself a '6' on his Emotional score. He is going through a difficult time in his life and he feels out of balance emotionally. John is having difficulties in his marriage and also with some of his teenage children. He feels a lot of pressure in his job and in his finances. He sometimes deals with this pressure emotionally.

Figure 1.8

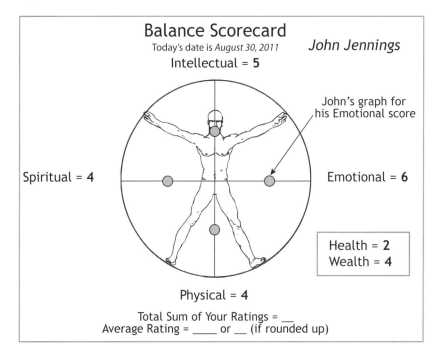

Balance Scorecard
Today's date is *August 30, 2011*   *John Jennings*
Intellectual = **5**

Spiritual = **4**   Emotional = **6**

John's graph for his Emotional score

Health = **2**
Wealth = **4**

Physical = **4**

Total Sum of Your Ratings = __
Average Rating = ____ or __ (if rounded up)

Step Five: Determine your balance score

To determine your Balance Score, take each of the ratings that you gave yourself above—Intellectual, Physical, Emotional and Spiritual—and add them up. The largest possible number is 40 (10 for each area) and the smallest possible number is 0 (0 for each area). Now divide this sum by 4 and you will get an overall assessment of your balance at this point in time, at whatever stage of life you are in. When you divide by 4, you

13

might get a decimal point in the answer. If you do, round up to the next largest whole number.

So in the example in Figure 1.9, the sum of John's scores is 19. 19 divided by 4 is 4.75. 4.75 rounded up to the next highest whole number is 5. So John's Balance Score is '5'. Remember that in the Balance Score, the largest possible score is '10' (where everything in life is out of balance) and the smallest possible score is '0' (where everything in life is in balance). Most people's scores will fall somewhere between '1' and '9'.

Figure 1.9

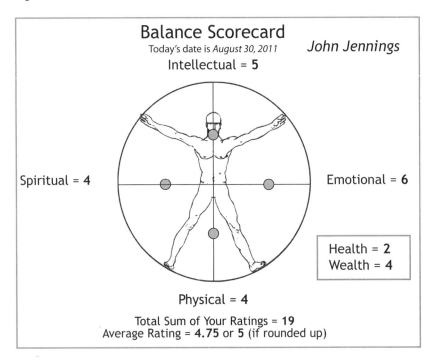

Balance Scorecard
Today's date is *August 30, 2011*   *John Jennings*
Intellectual = **5**

Spiritual = **4**   Emotional = **6**

Health = **2**
Wealth = **4**

Physical = **4**
Total Sum of Your Ratings = **19**
Average Rating = **4.75** or **5** (if rounded up)

Gretchen's assessment

Below is an assessment that one of my clients, Gretchen, made of herself. I said to her, "Let's start with your mind—your intellect. Are you in balance or are you out of balance? Do you need to learn some things?" She replied that she was somewhat out of balance and that she needed to take various training courses to bring her skills up to a new level. She rated herself a '5' on her Intellectual score. Then I asked her whether her health was in balance or out of balance. She replied that she is a '10' on her Health score. She is in constant pain and has a disease. Also her financial life was a complete disaster so she gave herself a '10' on her Wealth score. She determined that her overall Physical score is a '10'. I then asked her how she is spiritually—is she in balance or out of balance? Does she believe in God or in a Higher Being? She replied that yes, she believes in God and that she is "very mad" at Him. She gave herself a score of '10' on her Spiritual score. I then asked her the final assessment question on how she is emotionally. She replied that she is a '10' on her Emotional score and that she is an emotional "basket case." She then went on to tell me about some of the problems that she had in her life and how she was at that point being accused of doing some things that she never did. Her assessment is in Figure 1.10.

Figure 1.10

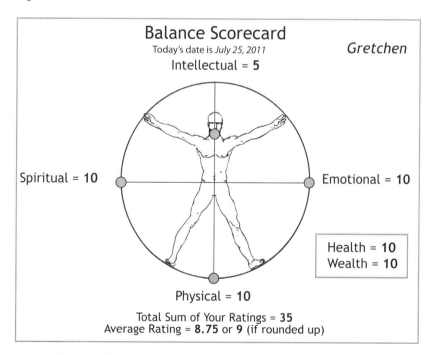

Notice that Gretchen is *way* out of balance. Here's the point: you can't renovate the house if the house is on fire! If everything is falling down around you, you can't concentrate on what is important. So we needed to assess how to get Gretchen back into balance *before* we looked at putting together a life plan that would move her from one place to another.

The Balance Scorecard tool presented here is an excellent tool. You can use it to determine your own life's balance. Balance sometimes changes based on conditions, so it is helpful to use this tool every few weeks to see where you are. This tool can also be used to figure out how to bring yourself back into balance.

> *You can't renovate the house if the house is on fire.*
> *First assess where you are. Determine how to get back*
> *into balance; then put together a life plan that will*
> *move you from one stage in your life to another.*

Step Six: Assess your score—look at where you are

After you have averaged each of the scores that you gave yourself and have come to an average rating, use the chart below as a gauge or a way to assess your own balance.

BALANCE SCORECARD

If you averaged between 0 and 3	You are probably pretty much in balance in your life—both with who you are and where you are in your life. You might want to make some minor adjustments to be even more in balance than you are now. However, you are in good shape and you might not need to make any balance changes at all. A good next step for you would be to see where you want to go next and to create a life plan to make this happen.
If you averaged between 4 and 7	You might be feeling a bit out of control; you might see people or events in your life as things that are pulling you out of balance. You might want to look at the various ratings that you gave yourself and ask yourself what you could do to change your current situation to put yourself back into balance. For instance, if you are out of balance physically, you might want to use your intellect (your mind) or your spirit to pull yourself back into balance. See what makes sense for you to bring more balance into your life.

If you averaged between 8 and 10

You might be feeling totally out of control; you might see things both inside and outside of yourself as a total mess. If this is the case, you might want to take a really hard look at what's happening in your life and take measures to immediately bring balance back into your life. You might be in some sort of crisis situation and you might not be thinking logically due to the pain that you are experiencing either from within yourself or from outside of yourself—or both. You might need to get immediate help. Think about what you can do to change the situation and to bring yourself back into more balance. Also think about what other people can do to help you. Going it alone right now might be very difficult and sharing the situation with others who can help might make a world of difference. One thing is for certain. You probably need to do something now to help yourself maintain some semblance of balance and control of your life.

Common actions needed to get back into balance

I have done hundreds of life plans. Here are some things that people have put down that they needed to do in each of the quadrants. I am giving the examples because they might be helpful to you and they might give you ideas on what you need to do for yourself.

Intellectual

- Take more classes
- Learn a foreign language
- Finish my degree
- Join a library group
- Focus and set goals for myself
- Expand the creative aspect of my life
- Enroll in a distance learning course
- Improve my English
- Think less; my mind is too overactive
- Calm my mind by meditating

Physical

- Buy a bicycle
- Take up a sport (yoga, martial arts, etc.)
- Eat more healthy foods
- Find a new living situation
- Change my job
- Lose weight
- Make more money
- Exercise
- Create a financial plan
- Quit smoking

Spiritual

- Journal
- Meditate
- Join a church or a spiritual community
- Figure out my life's purpose
- Make time to explore my Spirit
- Use music to uplift my Spirit
- Paint to uplift my Spirit
- Release my emotions through my Spirit
- Read metaphysical books
- Talk with God / the Universe regularly

Emotional

- Counterbalance through journaling & yoga
- Build my confidence
- Discern who I let into my life
- Fix my marriage
- Be sure that my needs are met
- Release the worry in my life
- Build a better support structure
- Find the love of my life
- Do active sports—like running, aerobics, etc.
- Assess my personal relationships
- Get professional help if needed
- Use my relationship with God to help me

John Jenning's filled-out Balance Worksheet
John Jenning's filled-out Balance Worksheet is in Figure 1.11. Notice how John has begun to sketch out some of the actions that he needs to take in order to bring himself back into balance. We will expand John's plan further as we delve more into this book.

Assess your own balance

Throughout this chapter I have encouraged you to assess yourself. If you are pretty much in balance you might not need to take any actions to maintain your balance. However, even the most balanced people continue to do certain things to maintain their balance. Ask yourself, if you *are* in balance, what keeps you there?

If you *are not* in balance, what do you need to do to bring yourself to *your* optimal balance? I encourage you to put together an assessment of your own balance and make a mini-action plan on what you need to do the get back into balance using the ideas presented in this chapter.

Figure 1.11

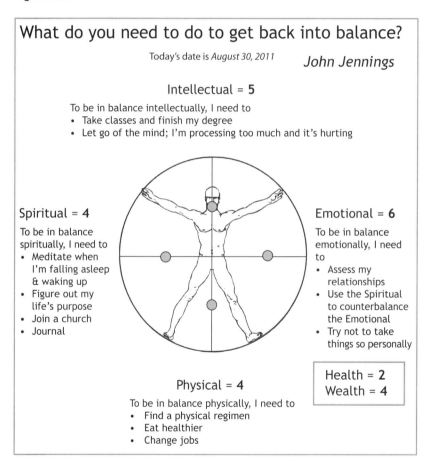

What do you need to do to get back into balance?

Today's date is *August 30, 2011*   *John Jennings*

Intellectual = **5**

To be in balance intellectually, I need to
- Take classes and finish my degree
- Let go of the mind; I'm processing too much and it's hurting

Spiritual = **4**

To be in balance spiritually, I need to
- Meditate when I'm falling asleep & waking up
- Figure out my life's purpose
- Join a church
- Journal

Emotional = **6**

To be in balance emotionally, I need to
- Assess my relationships
- Use the Spiritual to counterbalance the Emotional
- Try not to take things so personally

Physical = **4**

To be in balance physically, I need to
- Find a physical regimen
- Eat healthier
- Change jobs

Health = **2**
Wealth = **4**

Key Points

Reminders:

Do	Don't
▪ Look at your life every now and then to determine how in balance or out of balance you are. ▪ Remember the four main components to be in balance—our minds (Intellectual), our bodies' health (Physical - Health), our material world (Physical - Wealth), our relationship to something bigger than ourselves (Spiritual) and our feelings (Emotional). It is important to recognize each component and understand its role in your life. ▪ Remember to listen to your gut! It is usually right!	▪ Don't rush a life plan. Assess where you are and fix the situation if you are out of balance. Then put together a life plan that will move you from one place to another. ▪ Don't fool yourself when you are doing YOUR life plan. Answer the questions honestly; assess your current state as you believe it to be. If you do not like where you are, then let's make a plan to move you from here to there. The first step to do this is to figure out where you are NOW!

Scan the QR Code below to download your free Life Balance Self Help Test.

CHAPTER TWO:

Let's Talk About You
Your Core Values, Your Talents and Your Joys in Life

*Whenever you experience stress of any kind,
look into yourself and ask, "In what way am I
compromising my innermost values in this situation?"*

—Brian Tracy

Your core values

As you think about your life, think about your *core values*. Core values are what you believe and what you think is truly important to you as a person. These are not values that change from time to time, situation to situation or person to person, but rather they are the underpinnings of who you are and what you stand for. Think of them as those things you believe or want that are part of your core—the *inner* you.

When you ask yourself what your core values are, think about those things that are vital traits in yourself or in those whom you love and care about. Examples of things that are core values to people are honesty, friendship, loyalty, love, honor and trust. This is just to name a few; there are many, many others. The important question is "What is important to *you*?"

YOUR 'CORE VALUES' EXAMPLES

- A life centered around my family
- Earning a lot of money
- Belief in God and a life centered around God
- Being honest and associating with people who are honest
- Living a simple life, one without stress or frills

When you are building your life plan, it is important to understand what "makes you tick." By this I mean that you need to be clear about what really matters to you. If you don't think about this, you might make career choices, love choices and other choices that conflict with your core values. When people choose things that conflict with their core values, this puts them under a great deal of pressure and stress.

They feel torn between the thing that they are choosing and what they *really* believe and want.

> Core values *are what you believe and what you think is truly important to you as a person. ... They are the underpinnings of* who you are and what you stand for. *The important question is "What is important to* you?*"*

On a separate piece of paper, put the words My Core Values at the top of the page and list below it the traits in yourself or in other people that you value as important. Next to each core value, write *why* this value is important to you.

Your talents and your joys in life

When I do life planning sessions with people, too many times I hear the comment, "I don't have any talents." This just isn't true. Everyone has some talents. You were born with them. They are there. Some people don't perceive that they have them; others are very clear that they do. It is important that you think about what you are good at—even the small things.

Use those talents you have.
You will make it.
You will give joy to the world.
Take this tip from nature:
The woods would be a very silent place if no birds sang except those who sang best.

—Bernard Meltzer

So, let's brainstorm about you. Think about yourself. Think about your natural abilities, your talents. Think about what makes you happy and what gives you pure joy. Brainstorm how these talents can be used to make your life fuller or happier. When you do this brainstorming work, start by doing this exercise alone. Go into a quiet place, a place where you feel safe and happy. Think about your priorities, about your special skills and about the things in life that give you pure joy. When you are done with this exercise, feel free to share your thoughts with a trusted friend.

When you think about your talents, think too about those things that you were good at as a child—the things that came naturally to you then. Perhaps they are things that you have stopped doing in your adult life. Also think about all of the kinds of things that you are good at now—

some of the functions that you do at work, some of the things that you do at play or as hobbies, abilities that you have that come naturally to you. Here is a list of the kinds of things that people say when I do life plans for them:

'YOUR TALENTS' EXAMPLES:

- Good communicator
- Can take complex ideas and simplify them
- Great cook
- Good listener
- Great parent
- Good with hands and building things
- Good teacher
- Good singer
- Good at orchestrating events
- Loves the arts—performing, acting, singing, painting
- Good at organizing things
- Loves physical activities—to be outdoors
- Good at being a friend

On a separate piece of paper, put the words My Talents at the top of the page and list below it the areas where you are talented or have natural abilities. These are the things that you are good at doing.

Keep in mind that just because you are good at doing something doesn't mean that it gives you joy to do it. Many people have talents but the use of those talents might not fulfill them or give them happiness. I once did a life plan for an extremely successful businessman who made a lot of

Hide not your talents,
they for use were made.
What's a sun-dial in the shade?

—BENJAMIN FRANKLIN
(1706 - 1790)

money but was very unhappy in his life. Richard described himself as a "hamster running on the wheel of life." He was very good at making money. Every business undertaking he made turned to gold. He went from plane to plane, from meeting to meeting, and from phone call to phone call while his personal life disintegrated. His wife was unhappy, his children were distant, and he began to search for more meaning in life. As we did his life plan, Richard realized how out of balance he really was. His work consumed his life and his time. In his life plan, Richard chose to round himself out as a person, to not be so one-sided when it came to all work and no play. He chose to schedule more leisure and family time into his calendar. Little by little, Richard rebuilt his personal life. Today he is still making money but he is enjoying the fruits of his labor.

So now ask yourself what really gives you joy. What makes you happy in life? On a separate piece of paper, put the words "What Gives Me Joy in Life" at the top of the page and think of at least a dozen things in life that make you happy. Think about the two questions together—your talents and what gives you joy. If you match them together this is a good indicator of how you should spend your time. If you can spend a lot of time doing these things, your life will be happier. It really is up to you as to whether or not you give these things a priority in your life, but if you are good at certain things and they make you happy, it is reasonable to give them top priority. I have done life plans for people who have discovered that their everyday jobs do not match their talents and joys in life. In other life plans, people are doing exactly what they are talented at and what gives them joy in their full time job. If you find that your current job does not match what you are good at and what gives you joy, you can use the rest of this life planning methodology to build a plan to take you from where you *are* to where you *want to be*.

God doesn't give people talents that He doesn't want people to use.

—IRON EAGLE

You listed what your talents are and what gives you joy. Now examine the match of the two questions. Write down what talents you have that give you pure joy.

The importance of joy

I once heard a quote in a movie that said, "God is happiest when He sees His children at play." Do you think this is true and if you do, why do you think that it is true? Do you think that it is because *we're* happiest when we are at play? When you think about it, "play" is a very subjective word. Everyone has his or her own idea of what "to play" means to them. The act of playing is one of creation. When we play, we create an environment, a feeling, a material thing, an event or an action. Playing is a way for us to express ourselves. If you go with the notion that God or the Universe is always in the state of creation—of Being—then it falls into line that our expression of ourselves gives us joy, and it gives the Universe joy as well! The joy of creation has a natural "pull" to it. It gives us a sense of accomplishment and happiness and it actually draws abundance towards us. The act of creation sets the Universe in motion. We are not even conscious that we are doing this, and yet, the result is that we gain not only from the thing we created but from the whole process of creation and putting the Universe into motion for us.

Belief in our life situations

What do you believe about the situation that your life is in right now? Are you happy with where you are? Do you believe that you have to make "sacrifices"—maybe do things that you don't want to do or stay in a situation that you really don't like? Do you believe that life is a constant struggle? Do you believe that you have the power to change where you are into where you want to be?

God is happiest when He sees His children at play.

—The Legend of Baggar Vance

We human beings sometimes get caught in a spiral of pain. We don't like where we are but we just aren't sure how to change it. Sometimes people have some mistaken beliefs about life. The first mistake is that they think that constant struggle is okay—that we're supposed to work at a job we hate, doing things that take away our time, take away our lives and take away our youth—all just for making money and making ends meet. We're supposed to sacrifice all of the time. Isn't that what life is all about? Sacrifice? We're supposed to view fun as a little bonus—a little bone—that life throws to us every now and then. The second mistaken belief that people have is that you can't make money at the things that you enjoy, that they just don't pay or that because you enjoy them, they should be done for free. The third mistaken belief is that it is hard to change where we are in life to where we want to be.

Let's take the first mistaken belief—that sacrifice is a necessity in life—that the "rules" of life require us to slave away doing things that we don't enjoy just to make money. This idea just is not true. Of course we do things out of necessity, but we were created to have power over our lives, our minds, our thoughts and our experiences. We are the creators of our own realities. Think of the sun and sunbeams.

Work while you have the light. You are responsible for the talent that has been entrusted to you.

—Henri-Frédéric Amiel

The sunbeams are part of the sun. Each is a piece of the sun that has its own light. Now, think of God/the Universe and mankind. Each of us is a piece of God/the Universe and each of us has our own light. We are bright white lights that have the power to create! Wow! We can create good things for ourselves and conversely, we can create unhappy or bad things. Much of this creation is based on what we think. What this means is that where you are now is based on what you thought in the past. If you change your thinking now you can affect where you will be at some point in the future.

In the course of this book, we will address the second and third mistaken beliefs discussed above—that you can't make money at what you are good at and that you don't have the power to change any situation that you want.

> *You* can *make money at what you are good at and you* do *have the power to change any situation that you want.*

How all of our minds are connected together by a Universal Mind

Have you ever heard of negative mass consciousness? This is when groups of people start saying bad things and they come true. This could be about the economy being bad, the world situation being bad, how politics and the government can't be trusted, and companies aren't ethical. You get the idea. You see it everywhere on television and in the media. Watch any news channel and most of what you will see is about all of the terrible and sad events that happened during the day or week. Negative thoughts, negative ideas and negative statements are espoused constantly. Fear breeds fear. These thoughts are then increased by people telling other people, so that the negativity increases exponentially. The bad news eventually dies down until the next negative wave begins.

Let's start with a premise. Let's say that there is a Universal Mind that connects us all. Have you ever thought about someone whom you hadn't spoken with in years and then suddenly he or she calls out of the blue? I'll bet that this has happened to you many times in your life. This is because we are all mentally connected together by a Universal Mind. And what you think into this mind is what you get out of it.

As you are thinking about your life and what you want to do with it from here on out, it is important to think about what is important to you. It is important to think about your core values (who you are, what you believe, where you are strong), the talents that you have in life, and the things that give you joy.

Now you might ask how this ties in with your talents. When people say that they have no talents, in effect, they are bringing into reality a self-fulfilling prophecy. People who say they have no talents … presto magic, have no talents! What you *think* becomes true *for you*. Those who believe that they have no talents are usually also the ones who have a very negative self-image and a low self-esteem.

> *No one respects a talent that is concealed.*
>
> —DESIDERIUS ERASMUS

John Jenning's filled out 'Core Values, Talents and Joys' worksheet

Your Talents and Your Joys in Life Worksheet

What are your core values? What traits in yourself or in other people do you value as important?	
▪ Honesty ▪ Loyalty	▪ Family & friends

What are your core values? What traits in yourself or in other people do you value as important? Why are they important to you?	
Core Value / Trait	**Why is this important to you?**
▪ Honesty	▪ I want to be treated by others honestly—and this is how I treat them. When I'm not honest with myself, I get hurt.
▪ Loyalty	▪ I'm loyal to my family and friends
▪ Family & friends	▪ I have several life long friends. I value them as much as I value my family. I love to spend time with them.

What are your talents—your natural abilities? What are you good at doing?	
▪ Helping people ▪ Imaginative—artistic ▪ Writing	▪ Flexible ▪ Can look at the big picture ▪ Educating

What activities or things give you joy? What makes you happy?	
▪ Helping people ▪ Spending time with family ▪ Nature and outdoors ▪ Music	▪ Knowing that the people who you care about are well ▪ Things with passion and emotion ▪ Acts of kindness without recognition

Match the two questions above against each other. What talents do you have that give you pure joy?	
▪ Helping people ▪ Using my creativity in writing	▪ Creating awareness in others gives me a great sense of joy

Key Points

Reminders:

Do	Don't

• Think about your core values, your talents and what gives you joy in life. Match your talents and joys together and focus on spending time doing those things.
 	
• When we play, we tie into the creativity of the Universe and we bring abundance to ourselves and those around us.
 	
• Remember that you are very powerful. You have the power to create your world—whatever you want it to be. In fact, your current world has been created in the past by your thoughts, beliefs and actions.
	• Don't ever believe that you don't have talents. You were given talents when you were born and you've created more talents as you live.
	
	• Don't "buy in" to the three mistaken beliefs:
	  • Life has to be a constant struggle
	  • You can't make money doing what you're good at or what gives you pleasure
	  • You don't have the power to change things

CHAPTER THREE:

Your 'Self Talk' and the Power of Belief

We have only to believe. And the more threatening and irreducible reality appears, the more firmly and desperately we must believe. Then, little by little, we shall see the universal horror unbend, and then smile upon us, and then take us in its more than human arms.

—Pierre Teilhard De Chardin

We spoke in the last chapter about the Universal Mind and that the positive thoughts which go into Universal Mind produce positive results—and that negative thoughts which go into it, like negative mass consciousness, produce negative outcomes and results in our world and in our lives. If we think of Universal Mind as a giant computer that reflects back to us what is put into it, this comes close to what I believe is actually happening. Let's go further into the concept of our thoughts and beliefs and that we can change or shape our environment and our lives.

When we think, we subconsciously tie into Universal Mind. This is the thought structure—the link or the glue—that ties us all together. We might not know it is there but it is real and what we think *into* it has effect. Our thoughts have a way of coming true—and our reality can then be perceived by us as "good", "neutral" or "bad." It all depends on what you think about your situation. Your perception is your reality.

The Universe doesn't judge what comes into it; it produces an output that matches the input that it was given. Did you ever hear people say "I'm sick and I'm tired," and they are always sick and they are always tired? Conversely, have you ever noticed people who just never seem to get down, even when they are faced with difficult situations? They just keep on going and the bad things that they face eventually go

Whatever you accept into your mind has reality for you. It is your acceptance that makes it real.

—*A Course in Miracles*

away while good things seem to come to them very often. When you look at them, you might think that they are very lucky, but in reality it is more than luck. It is an alignment with the Universe.

> *Think of Universal Mind as a giant computer*
> *that reflects back to us what is put into it. ...*
> Your perception is your reality.

Cause and effect

We have all seen cause and effect in our lives. This is how it works: I do something and then an event happens. I cause it to happen by my actions. A very simple example of this is a physical one where I strike a match (cause) and I get fire (effect). Cause and effect happens so much in the physical side of life that we tend to take them for granted. I drop a ball (cause) and it falls to the ground through gravity (effect). When I push a button, a bell rings.

What a lot of people do not recognize, though, is that cause and effect goes beyond the physical nature of life and extends into the mental and spiritual nature of life as well. Our thoughts actually bring people, events and things towards us. As stated in the last chapter, I used the example of how you could think of someone whom you hadn't thought about for a long time and then suddenly that person calls you on the phone. Also as stated previously, the things that we attract to us can be good or bad, depending on our thoughts, beliefs and our perception of them. Two people can see the same thing. One person can perceive this thing as *good*; another person can perceive it as *bad*.

The words and ideas that run through our minds are very important ... what we are "telling ourselves" in our minds is the basis on which we form our experience of reality.

—SHAKTI GAWAIN,
CREATIVE VISUALIZATION

The strength of your thoughts and beliefs actually determines the power of the result. If you believe strongly and take action to make "it" happen (whatever it is), it most likely will eventually come true. It all depends on your belief, your desire, your actions and your alignment with the Universe. The Universe honors us by fulfilling or manifesting what we think into it. The big secret in this life is that we have the power to create and bring things to ourselves. But most of us don't know that we have any power at all!

Thoughts are things. When we think something, we actually create it. Sometimes it takes time for this thing of our thoughts—this output— to manifest. It isn't always immediate. Sometimes though, the thought manifests into a tangible real thing immediately. Two things throw us off. The first is that we don't always understand that our thoughts are things and that our thoughts actually create experiences, events, materials things, emotions—you name it. Due to this, we don't always understand how powerful our minds *really* are. The second is that we have conditioned ourselves to expect immediate results or consequences when we take action. We are so conditioned by immediate cause and effect, like when dropping a ball. Because we associate cause and effect with mostly the physical world—which usually brings about immediate results—we don't consider that our thoughts actually trigger events that might *not* happen immediately. Sometimes it takes the Universe time to manifest what we're thinking. If we think of the Universe as a giant computer working on a complex problem, it works in a logical progression—where sometimes solutions come immediately and sometimes they come in time.

> *The big secret in this life is that we have the power to create and bring things to ourselves. Most of us don't know that we have any power at all!*

And actually, this is a blessing. Imagine what your life would be like if you thought something and it happened immediately. You might need to control every thought—because things might happen that you really don't want to happen! I'm sure that you've heard the old saying, "Be careful what you wish for." By not delivering immediate results all of the time, the Universe gives us a chance to be *very* sure what we *really* want!

> *Our thoughts are extremely powerful! You have much more power over your life than you know!*

Sometimes people tell me that they are very sure what they want and that the Universe has not delivered it to them. However, when we speak about this desired result, some of the people express confusion about what they *really* want. They want this, but they don't want that. They want it to be exactly this way, but maybe it might be better another way. When we are confused as to what we want, then so is the Universe. If we straddle a fence and are not clear, the Universe usually does not deliver.

> *When we are confused as to what we want—*
> *so is the Universe.*

The power of belief

There is a famous quote that is attributed to Napoleon Hill, which goes like this: "What the mind of man can conceive and believe, it can achieve." What this means is that our thoughts are extremely powerful! So if you say things to yourself like, "I am smart. I am capable. I am talented (in a certain area). I am successful" and you *believe* these statements, they will come true—in time. The key factor here is to think and to believe and to allow the Universe to deliver the result when IT sees fit, not when we demand the result to occur.

What the mind of man can conceive and believe, it can achieve.

—NAPOLEON HILL

Did you ever see the movie *Gone with the Wind*? At one point, Scarlett O'Hara has just been through the surrender of Atlanta to the Union Army and she barely manages to get herself and her friend, Melanie, to her home at Tara. When she arrives at Tara, everything is a disaster. Her mother is dead; her father has gone insane and the rest of the family is starving. Exhausted beyond belief and at her breaking point, Scarlett raises her fist to the sky as she declares to the Universe, "I'll never be hungry again!" Here Scarlett is making a contract with the Universe. She knows deep down inside herself that she would *never, ever* be hungry again. She will do anything that she has to do to avoid that outcome. Her words and her belief had the power to change the external circumstances and events in her life.

The same holds true for us. We have the power to change our circumstances. We have the power to change the events in our lives that we don't like. We have the power to direct good things to come to us. The key to all of this power lies in our thoughts, in our minds and in our beliefs.

This is why "self-talk" is so important. This is why what you put into your mind is important to your wellbeing. This includes things like what you see, what you read, what you hear, what you watch on television or in the movies. You can put anything into your mind but if you fill it with negative thoughts and negative ideas about yourself and the world, you will see and perceive a lot of negative things happening all around you, to both you and those you love. But, if you fill your mind with positive beliefs about yourself, your family, your friends, your coworkers, and the people of the world, you will begin to see positive events come into your life.

> *If you develop the absolute sense of certainty that powerful beliefs provide, then you can get yourself to accomplish virtually anything, including those things that other people are certain are impossible.*
>
> —ANTHONY ROBBINS

This is much more than the power of positive thinking. It is a Law of the Universe—the Law of Universal Mind. We are all tied together as human beings by our minds and by our thoughts. We, as human beings, have so much more in common than we have things that separate us. Our thoughts and ideas can be used for positive, powerful, constructive reasons and results—or they can be used for pain and destruction.

> *Our life is what our thoughts make it.*
>
> —MARCUS AURELIUS ANTONIUS

Personally, I am not a masochist! I prefer positive things to happen to me and to my family, so I use my mind to bring good things to myself and to those around me. This comes about from my "self-talk." My self-talk is what I tell myself in the private confines of my mind. It's what I bring to myself in my quiet time in meditation as I am working my way through the things that have happened to me today or the new ideas that have come to me.

Recently two of the people for whom I did life plans were having financial difficulties in their lives. One said to me, "My back hurts and I wonder if this is because I can't support myself." The other said, "You know, my knees hurt and I wonder if it is because I can't stand on my own two feet financially." I think it is interesting how our minds and bodies work together. Sometimes one problem can manifest itself as another problem. Let's look at the metaphors that appeared in these two people's lives. Financially, they were both in very difficult situations. Their minds could very easily have manifested bodily ills through their use of words, thoughts and beliefs. When we say to ourselves, "I can't support myself," the mind can very easily manifest a physical problem in the body and it could turn up as a literal, physical situation of "I can't support myself," so my back will now hurt. The same with the phrase, "I can't stand on my own two feet financially." This can translate from the mind to the body into a problem with the knees. Think about it. Is one situation in your life causing other problems in other aspects of your life?

So when we fill our minds with negative thoughts, we attract negative things to ourselves. Some people call this the Law of Attraction. Conversely, when we fill our minds with positive thoughts, we attract positive things to ourselves. Have you ever noticed how you might get "bad vibes" from certain people? They exude an aura or a feeling that makes you uncomfortable and you feel repelled. You stay away from them. Conversely, there might be other people who attract you; their very presence brings you to them. You feel comfortable with their thoughts, with their demeanor and with their aura. You are pulled towards them. The questions we always need to ask ourselves are: "What am I thinking?" "What am I projecting?" "What am I bringing toward myself?" "What do I choose to pull into myself from the Universe?"

You are a living magnet. What you
attract into your life is in harmony
with your dominant thoughts.

—BRIAN TRACY

Bring the things that you want to yourself: the "Drain/Gain" exercise
When I do life plans for people, I give them a process that truly brings them all of the things in life that they want. This process really works! Try it for yourself! The process is called the "Drain/Gain" exercise. Do the exercise twice a day, at night and in the morning. It needs to be done when you are in half-sleep—just when you are waking up and just as you are about to fall asleep. I call this state of grogginess "la-la land."

First, start by imagining that you are on a beach at low tide. The gentle surf laps at your feet as the waves recede. The air smells fresh and salty. The water has created tide pools and you are standing in one as the water is pulling, almost as if you are in a vacuum. Feel the sand and the water pulling at your feet and allow the sand to drain *all* negative energy from your body. Think of yourself as a gas tank and start the draining from the top of your head and allow it to be released through your feet. Say to yourself, "I am draining negative energy from my head. I am draining negative energy from my eyes. I am draining fear. I am draining worry. I am draining negative thinking." Actually feel it moving down, down, down, all the way down your body. Relax but don't fall asleep yet. When you get down to your feet, you will feel empty but still don't fall asleep! (If you do, don't worry, try again the next day.)

Second, once you are "empty," imagine that you are a tree. You have roots that go into the ground and branches that reach to the sky. Pull positive energy into yourself from God/the Universe asking to be filled with all the good things that you desire—perfect health, happiness, peace, love, joy—abundance of all kinds. Now, imagine that the Universe is "filling you up" with these things. When we fill a container, the liquid goes into the bottom of the container and then it fills up to the top. The good things will start from your feet. Consciously pull the good things into yourself. Pull them up and into your body—to your knees, to your stomach, and so on.

If you think of the Universe and of Infinity, you will be thinking of the enormity of both God and the Universe. Think of yourself as a bright white light—as perfection—as God and the Universe are perfect. Bring good things to yourself. Think about drawing them into yourself, into your life. Visualize the power that you have and fill yourself up with the bright white light. This might be the most important step of them all.

Third, when you get to your heart area, if you believe in God or a deity or someone special to you who has passed on, put that deity or person in front of you. Let that image spin these things into you, so that the result is ever increasing from them to you to them and so forth. This "spinning" builds up the intensity and duration of receiving the gifts from the Universe that you desire.

Fourth, if it's at night, then go to sleep. Your subconscious mind will pull these things to you while you sleep. It is as if you have programmed your subconscious mind to work out how to get the things to you that you have requested. Remember, the Universe is like a giant computer—it will deliver "like" to "like." Good, positive thoughts will produce good, positive results. Negative thoughts will produce negative results. In the old computer programming days, there was an adage "Garbage in … garbage out." This not only goes for programming computers. It goes for programming your mind.

If you're doing this in the morning (remember "la-la land," the half sleep before you're fully awake), do the same process as described above, but as the fourth step, ask the Universe to tell you the two to three things that you need to do for this day. Just let the answers come to you. Do them and then you've done what you need to do for the day. Your work, as far as the Universe is concerned, is done.

Now wait and have faith in God/the Universe, but keep doing the technique until you get what you want. This technique *works*. Bring in a new job for yourself. Bring in a new boss. Bring in a promotion. Bring in money. Whatever … just "pull" all of it to you.

I was doing a business planning session in China. In my session, the Chinese customers asked me how I have so much energy. I described the technique to them that I just described to you. I told them how I visualize myself as a tree in the morning before I get up and I ask God/the Universe to deliver the energy and words to me that I need for them. I ask the Universe to please help me to help them—that I have the words, the power and the energy when I need it. I fill my self with positive energy and power. As I described the process, one of the colleagues said to me, "Do you know that you are doing a form of T'ai Chi?" I replied, no, I didn't—I was just using a technique that I had created because it felt natural and correct to me.

The reason man may become
the master of his own destiny is
because he has the power to influence
his own subconscious mind.

—Napoleon Hill

The 'Drain/Gain' exercise steps

Step 1	Imagine that you're on a beach with your feet close enough to the shore so that the waves just reach your feet. Feel the "pull" of the water in the sand as the waves recede—as if you are in a vacuum. Allow this pull to drain all of the negative energy from you. Let it drain out from the bottom of your feet into the soft sand into the earth where it will be burned up in the fires of the earth's core. Start the draining of this negative energy from the top of your head and work your way systematically down each part of your body. Try not to fall asleep.
Step 2	Now imagine that you are a tree. You have roots going deep into the earth and branches reaching up into the sky. Pull in the positive things that you desire for yourself. This is the "gain." Fill yourself up like an empty vessel so that the goodness fills from the bottom of your feet to the top of your head. Systematically move up your body as you "fill" yourself with what you desire.
Step 3	When you get to your heart area, allow a deity or someone special to you to "spin" the positive energy from them to you and back to them again. Build up the power and momentum of the "spin."
Step 4	If it's night time, go to sleep and allow God/the Universe to work in your subconscious mind to deliver these things to you. If it's the morning, ask the Universe the 2-3 things that you need to do today. Do them and then you have done what you're supposed to do.

Listening to your Higher Self

Do you know that you have a "Higher Self"? Do you know that there is a *you* bigger than the "you" that you experience in your everyday life? The Higher You is your Higher Self. You can learn to access the "Higher You" to give you guidance or to tell you what to think or say. The Higher You comes across to us as a voice in our heads. The Bible calls it the "still, small voice." Sometimes people say, "I don't hear a voice inside of me. I have no idea what this means." Well, I'll give you times when you absolutely hear yourself speak. How about when the pit of your stomach drops when you know that something is wrong?

How about when you drop something—or you make a mistake—and you feel a lurch in your stomach at the time that this event takes place? Perhaps you ignore your stomach to find out later that when you felt the uneasiness in the pit of your stomach was actually when the negative event happened. How about when you talk to yourself and you hear yourself speak? Maybe the "self" you hear speak is wiser than you. It gives you good advice and it warns you when something is going wrong. This is your Higher Self.

If you accept that you have a Higher You, you might be asking yourself why this is important. What good is a Higher Self and what does it do for you? Your Higher Self actually ties you into the Universe and Universal Mind. Your Higher Self uncovers the truth about what is real and what is going on. Your Higher Self provides you with the true situation; it cuts out all of the illusion that you might see in this world. If you listen to it, it can guide you through life and it can help you avoid pitfalls and obstacles. It can lead you to your right path. It can protect you. It is *very* powerful. It is the big YOU guiding the small "you" that is here on this earth.

If you are a mentally sane person and you listen to the Higher You, you will find out that there is much more "sanity" inside of you than there is outside out of you. Let's face it: sometimes this world seems insane. If you judge the world based on what we all see on television, you will believe that this world is only filled with disharmony, violence and chaos. However, if you go "inside" yourself and listen to your Higher Self, you will hear a voice of reason—a voice of sanity and calm. Which would you rather listen to—the voice of calm and reason on the inside or the very noisy voices of disharmony and chaos on the outside?

Every waking moment we talk to ourselves about the things we experience. Our self-talk, the thoughts we communicate to ourselves, in turn control the way we feel and act.

—JOHN LEMBO

The power of "I AM" statements

When I do this portion of the methodology with clients, I don't give them time to think. I "spring it" on them. I take the pen out of their hands and I ask them to allow me to take control of the pen. I tell them that I will write down every word that they say. I just want them to sit back and relax and I'll fill in the blanks. I want them to answer from their gut and I want them to give me all of the words that they can think of to describe themselves until they run out of steam. I ask them to just fill in the statement, "I am _____." Okay ... GO!

Try this for yourself. Please don't read ahead and do not overanalyze this exercise. Just sit down in a quiet place before you do this. Take a blank piece of paper and a pen. Write down the words, "I am _____" then quickly write down all of the words that come into your mind. *Do not* give it much thought; just fill in the blanks.

What did you actually say about yourself? What do you really think about yourself? What is your "self-talk" like? What kinds of adjectives did you use to describe yourself? Were they positive and self-empowering? Or, were they negative or self-limiting?

Now, analyze the statements that you just made about yourself. Sort through them and ask yourself which statements are positive and which are negative. Understand that the value judgment that you give as to whether something is positive and empowering or negative and self-limiting is totally up to you. Answer the positive or negative aspects of the statements from your gut, your intuition. Let your "gut feel" tell you which are positive and which are not.

Now, ask yourself if you need to rethink some of the negative or self-limiting statements that you made about yourself. Are they really true about you or did someone else influence you over the course of your lifetime with them? Let me give you an example. I did a life plan for a woman, who when asked to give her statements, said "I am worthless." As we went through her life plan, I asked her about that statement. Apparently it was her father's nickname for her when she was young and she grew up believing it. So when we delved into her core beliefs about herself, many of the thoughts and images of worthlessness and low self-esteem showed up in her statements. I then asked her, "So, was your father right? Are you really worthless?" She replied, "No, I am not!" This caused her to go into deep reflection on her beliefs about herself and her self worth.

> *If you're not all right the way you are*
> *it takes a lot of effort to get better.*
> *Realize that you're all right the way you are,*
> *and you'll get better naturally.*
> *Don't change beliefs.*
> *Transform the believer.*
>
> —WERNER ERHARD

Guilt, fear, projection and judgment

Sometimes we see things in ourselves that we do not like and many times we see the exact same things in other people. We actually project our perceived "faults" or "failings" onto these people and the perceived "failings" or "faults" then become exaggerated to the point where they become glaringly obvious and irritating to us. Other observers might not see these "failings" or "faults" at all.

As we project onto others, the vicious cycle continues on and on as we set ourselves up for more rejection, pain and fear. But what is fear? In some instances, fear is totally justified—like if we feel a physical threat of some sort and our gut tells us that there is real danger ahead. In other instances, though, the fear is not real. It is perceived as FEAR (False Evidence Appearing Real). As we FEAR, we "see" things, and in "seeing" these things, we project guilt and blame onto them. Fear, Uncertainty and Doubt (FUD) then drive us to judgment of either ourselves or others.

Whether we project blame onto others or onto ourselves, we may be judging unfairly. We put the "guilty parties" into our own mental court system where we try them, we bring false evidence and witnesses against them and then we convict them. As we find them guilty by projection, we find ourselves guilty as well—but guilty of what? Of what other people think of us? Guilty of our own feelings of failure? Guilty of what we should have done or could have done? Guilty of who we are or what we believe? What are we *actually* guilty of? In many cases, *nothing*!

Low self-esteem and self doubt

Think of the spiral of low self-esteem playing upon itself to intensify into constant self doubt. Low self-esteem can be brought on by other people telling a person that he or she is "not enough"—not smart enough, not pretty enough, not good enough—as in the case of the woman I mentioned above. As she heard the comments long enough and often enough, she bought into them, thereby producing her low self-esteem. Her father's treatment of her was mental/emotional abuse. Low self-esteem can also be brought on by physical abuse. Low self-esteem leads to constant self doubt.

My brother is a doctor. One day he had a patient with very low self-esteem. He asked her, "Do you care what other people say about you?" She said, "No, I don't care." He replied, "Then why do you care about what *you* say about yourself?" She replied, "You know, you're right." With this story in mind, I ask us all to go one step further and to forgive others and to forgive ourselves—because this might be where the core of the problem lies.

Forgiveness

Sometimes it is hard to forgive—especially when we feel that we have been wronged. If you have a belief system that embraces guilt and retribution then it will be extremely hard for you to forgive. In this belief system, vengeance is justified. However, if you have a belief

If you could really accept that you weren't ok
you could stop proving you were ok.
If you could stop proving that you were ok
you could get that it's ok not to be ok.
If you could get that it's ok not to be ok
you could get that you were ok the way
you were. You're ok, get it?

—WERNER ERHARD

system that says that we are not bodies—that we *have bodies but we are not bodies*—then forgiveness can be easier. This belief system says that we are spirits in bodies who are on this earth to learn and that this world is a giant school. In any learning situation, we make mistakes. That is the nature of a school—to makes mistakes and hopefully to learn from them. If we don't learn from our mistakes, have you ever noticed how the Universe keeps bringing the same learning situation (maybe in a different form) back again and again until we "get it" and we learn the lesson? If you can buy into this belief system, then forgiveness is easier.

My friend, Irit, is Jewish. She feels that the word "forgiveness" is too Christian. I asked her, "Irit, if you didn't use the word, 'forgiveness', what would you use?" She replied, "Love, Mary, love. It's all about love." Irit is right. It really is all about love.

So as we grow, mature and evolve into enlightened beings, we come across different learning situations which lead us to our current thoughts and beliefs. Over time our thoughts and beliefs may change. My advice to us all is "Keep whatever serves you. Release whatever does not." This includes all physical things, feelings, thoughts or beliefs that you might possess. Only keep what serves you and what leads you to the Higher You. Release the others.

Keep whatever serves you. Release whatever does not.

Why are you here on this earth? What is your mission in life?

When I do life plans with people, I ask them to think about why they are here on this earth—what their mission in life is. I ask them to think about their epitaph—what they would want their obituary to say or what they would want on their tombstone. A wise man once said to write your own eulogy and then work backwards to change your life story. This might sound morbid, but it's not. We need to ask ourselves what we want to accomplish on this earth for the remainder of the time that we have here. Our short-term goals tend to change over time. We set an objective for ourselves, we accomplish it and then we move on to the next goal. However, the mission of our lives is broader than a short-term goal. It is the reason why we are here. It is what "drives" us throughout our lives. It is almost as if we agreed to take on a role or responsibility— that we agreed to achieve something before we were born. It is as if our Higher Selves direct us towards accomplishing that "thing," whatever it is. Sometimes we listen and we feel good because we are doing what we're supposed to be doing. Sometimes we flounder and we feel frustrated that we're stalling. We know that we are supposed to be doing something but we are not sure what that "something" is.

It is important for people to reflect on why they think that they are here on this earth. Many times their core values, their talents and their joys actually set them up to accomplish what they are intended to do. We need to pay attention to the gifts that we are given because those gifts are what can and should be used to move us to the next level of our lives— the next plane of our existence.

Cherish forever what makes you unique,'cuz you're really a yawn if it goes.

—BETTE MIDLER

I get so many varied mission statements from people when I do their life plans. Let me give you some examples:

- My life's purpose is to help my Dad in his journey while he was alive. And now that he is dead, I still feel that I am still helping him. My life's purpose is also to help kids.
- My life's purpose is to be happy, to enjoy life. The world is a better place because I'm here. I'm living a good life, a happy life.
- My life's purpose is to find out who I am. I'm a soul that needs to have a human experience—to gain, to lose, to leave the world in better shape because of what I've done.
- I don't know what my mission in life is but I know God does have a reason for me to be here.

- My mission in life is to be a good mother and my life's purpose is to read people.
- I'm a sunbeam—unpredictable and lively—a thing that dances. I'm here to enjoy people and make them feel warm, to brighten them up when they feel dull.
- In the short term, my mission in life is to provide for my children and to make their childhood happy. In the long term, my mission in life is that I have something to say to and for the world.

Now, ask yourself, why are you here on this earth? What is your mission statement for your life? What is your Life's Purpose?

> *You are a powerful, creative person,*
> *able to do, be and have what you want in life;*
> *able to do what you love,*
> *and to do it in your own way.*
>
> —MARC ALLEN, *THE MILLIONAIRE COURSE*

What is your Mission in Life? ...
Why are you here on this earth? ...
What do you NEED to do? ...
What is Your Life's Purpose?

Scan the QR Code below to buy Marc Allen's fabulous book,
The Greatest Secret of All Time.

John Jenning's filled-out "What you SAY about yourself" worksheet

What do you say about yourself? What do you believe? What does your "self-talk" sound like? Don't overanalyze this. Just quickly fill in the blank: I AM _____	
▪ Happy	▪ Confident
▪ Successful	▪ Trustworthy
▪ Erratic—can be very self critical	▪ Critical and judgmental
▪ I have something to give	▪ A good listener
▪ Perfectionist	▪ Likeable
▪ Kind	▪ Thorough
▪ Caring	▪ Honest
▪ Generous	▪ Loyal
▪ Loving	▪ A good father

Which of the statements above are positive and empowering?	
▪ Happy	▪ Confident
▪ Successful	▪ Trustworthy
▪ I have something to give	▪ A good listener
▪ Kind	▪ Likeable
▪ Caring	▪ Thorough
▪ Generous	▪ Honest and Loyal
▪ Loving	▪ A good father

Which of the statements above are negative or self limiting?	
▪ Erratic—can be very self critical	▪ Critical and judgmental
▪ Perfectionist	of others

Are there any beliefs that you must rethink because you are selling yourself short or these beliefs are hurting you in some way?	
▪ I'm sometimes too hard on myself. I need to give myself more of a break	▪ Because I'm so hard on myself, I'm sometimes too hard on others
	▪ I need to lighten up a bit

What is your Mission Statement for your life? What is your Life's Purpose? Why are you here on earth?	
▪ To bring together different people, things and events— allowing people to move forward in their lives	▪ To get the stories I've written and told into movies and books

Key Points

Reminders:

Do	Don't
• Take the time to think through what you say about yourself. Listen to yourself. Listen to your self-talk. Catch yourself saying something—whether it's "positive" or "negative" about yourself.	• If you find yourself saying something negative about yourself, don't beat yourself up. Don't put more pressure on yourself than you already have. Ask yourself why you think what you think and then ask yourself how you can change this belief. Remember that your "gut" is your barometer. LISTEN TO YOURSELF. LISTEN TO THE INNER "YOU"—YOUR HIGHER SELF. The Higher YOU will tell you what to do next. When you go deep down inside yourself, trust yourself above all others and above all else. When you are deep inside yourself you are talking with God/the Universe.
• Ask yourself—"What do I really believe about ME?"	
• Take the time every day to release the negative energy from your body and spirit and bring in the positive energy from the Universe by doing the "Drain/Gain" exercise.	
• Think about why you are here in this world, in this life. Combine your core values, your talents and your joys in life with what you say about yourself and what you believe about yourself. Assess where you are and then start thinking and dreaming about what you choose next for yourself.	• Don't listen to the "noise" of negativity. Don't repeat the negative statements that you have heard or accepted before now. Examine your beliefs and decide which beliefs serve you.

CHAPTER FOUR:

What do You Dream about Doing?

Yes, you can be a dreamer and a doer too, if you will remove one word from your vocabulary: impossible.

—H. Robert Schuller

What are your dreams?

Think about what you want to have happen. What do you choose for yourself? Dream and dream big. Visualize yourself doing whatever makes you truly happy, deep-down-inside happy. Where are you? Who are you with? What is around you? What are you doing? Now express this dream as best fits you and your personality.

I spoke earlier about how people use the left or right lobes of their brains to make decisions. Many times when we analyze, we draw upon the left lobe of our brains to process the data and come to conclu-

If you can DREAM it, you can DO it.

—Walt Disney

sions. When we do artistic things we draw more upon the right lobe of our brains to create forms of expression. When we daydream, we tend to draw more upon the right lobe than the left lobe of our brains in the creation of our *play world*.

At this point in the methodology, I ask the question "What do you dream about?" Some people start by writing down their ideas. "I am (doing the following) _____." (State where you are, with whom, doing what, what you are seeing, feeling, hearing, etc.). By answering this question, these people are using the left lobe of their brains to brainstorm about what they are doing. I ask them to continue this brainstorm and to make this as real as possible for themselves.

After they've written down what they see themselves doing, I hand them four or five colored markers and a piece of paper. I ask them to take their time and draw/express their dream—what they *see* for themselves. I tell them that it is very important that they put themselves into the dream. Some people say to me, "I can't draw." I reply, "That's okay. The Universe honors stick figures. It knows what you mean. Just draw. Express yourself. Put yourself into the picture. Use diagrams, use flowcharts, use pictures—use anything that expresses what you see for yourself and about yourself. You must put YOU into the picture and it needs to be in color because the world is in color."

When we draw our dreams, as when we daydream, we tend to utilize the right lobe of our brains to create what we want. Some people make collages of what they dream about. Others just use a photograph of something that they want very much. I know of a woman who really wanted a certain house that she had seen in a local magazine. She said to her husband, "Bill, I want that house." Her husband said, "Mary, that house is too expensive; there is no way that we can afford it." Mary replied, "I don't care, Bill. I really want that house." Mary put the photo of the house on the mantle in her bedroom and she passed it every day. Sometimes she noticed it, and sometimes she didn't notice it. After about nine months, Mary asked Bill to go to an Open House that was advertised in the newspaper. It was in a neighboring town that she liked very much. They went to the Open House and when they got there Bill said "Mary, this is your house." Mary replied, "No it's not." Bill said, "Mary, this is your house, the house on the mantle. This is your house." Mary did not realize that the house in the Open House was *her* house—the house of her dreams—the house on her mantle. What she also did not realize is that the Universe manifested her dream for her. By the time that Bill and Mary physically got to the Open House, the house had been on the market for a long time. The owner of the house was "house rich" and "cash poor." The owner had come down significantly in price and Mary got the house of her dreams.

Shoot for the moon.
Even if you miss, you'll land
among the stars.

—Les Brown

That is why it is so important to put your dreams down on paper—to visually see them. By drawing your dreams, the dream expresses itself from your mind, from your heart, from your gut, through your hand, onto the paper and then into the Universe. It's amazing. The drawing of the dream in essence creates your contract with the Universe. You can use other forms of expression beyond drawings. A collage, photos, something written, anything created by you will do the job. All you need to do is express yourself and your desires first. The Universe really wants to give you what you want! Again, think of the Universe as a giant computer. What you put in is what you get out. Its job is to manifest—to bring into being—your thoughts, your ideas, your truest desires, your goals.

What happens when we have conflict over what we want?

The problem that people face is when they really don't know what they want. They think that they want a certain thing but deep down inside, they really don't want it—or they might not be sure that they want it. It's sort of like a tug of war: I want it. I don't want it. I want it. I don't want it. If you're confused, the Universe will be confused on your behalf. When things stall, when we don't get what we think that we want, we need to analyze what we're really telling the Universe. Do we *really* want that thing? Or are we saying we want it but deep down inside us we fear having it for some reason or another?

Let me give you an example. I did a life plan for a man named Roger who made an "I am" statement as follows: "I am wealthy in all non-worldly things." When I asked Roger if any of his "I am" statements were negative or self-limiting, he said, "No, I don't think that any of these statements are a problem." Roger's "reality" was that his life was filled with constant money worries and struggles. I then asked Roger what he believed about money. Roger said that he thought that money was an evil thing. Yet, in his dreams, he dreamt of having enough money to live a comfortable life with his family. I asked Roger if he saw a conflict there. He was telling the Universe that he wants money but that he really doesn't want it because he perceives it as being evil. In essence, Roger was telling the Universe, "I want money. I don't want it. I want it. I don't want it. Why haven't you given it to me?"

Roger was confused about how he felt about money. He was doing a tug of war within himself. He was so frustrated about things stalling that he did not realize that he was giving a mixed message to the Universe. *When we are confused, it's as if the Universe is confused as well.* It doesn't know what to give us so it gives us nothing. This is when things in our world stall and it feels as if the Universe has stalled. So if you are stalled but you really want to move forward in some way, ask yourself if you are confused between your *wants* and your *core beliefs*. Be clear about what you want and be really clear that you *really* want it. Is there a conflict there or mixed thoughts of some sort that are keeping you from getting what you really want? Look inside yourself and listen to the innermost part of your being. There you will find what you truly desire.

The role of our core values and our core beliefs

We just spoke of conflict and what happens when you aren't really sure about what you want. Let's go a bit further on core values and core beliefs. The man who I described above, Roger, believed that money is evil. He had a negative image of an inanimate object. Money is a thing. It has no feelings. It is neither good nor bad. People can use it for good purposes and people can use it for evil purposes. It can be acquired by honorable means and it can be acquired by dishonest and unethical means. I like to think of money as a thing—like air and water are things. I expect clean air. I expect good water. I don't have emotions about the air or the water. I expect them to be there. Why do we put value judgments on inanimate objects? They are really just things that can be used for any purpose that we desire.

Sometimes people tend to believe in "lack." They believe that there isn't enough stuff to go around. There isn't enough money, there isn't enough business, there isn't enough love—name "it." They believe that there just isn't enough of "it." What this leads to is a *lack* mentality. They are constantly trying to catch up and overcome the lack of this or that. They believe that life is a battle and that you need to overcome lack and fight for what you need and what you want. Life is not a zero sum game. What this means is that if you attain something that does not mean that someone else has to lose. The wins and losses in life do not need to equal zero!

A better way to look at life is to think that there is enough of everything for everyone. You don't need to fight. You don't need to overcome the next guy who is your competition for this or for that. You don't need to be on the floor bleeding, begging the Universe or God to give you what you want or need. You just need to allow the abundance of the Universe to come to you and to fill you. I am not saying here that you shouldn't compete in a business situation. Yes, indeed, you should compete honestly and ethically, showing the customer why you are the best choice for them. Inside yourself know that the Universe is "for" you—it wants for you what you *really* want. My husband has commented many times that in sports situations, the team that wants and needs the win the most gets it—they win. So too with the Universe. If you *really* want something, the Universe wants to give it to you. It wants to give you its full gifts—the gifts of health, happiness, peace, love, joy and abundance of all good things.

As Roger analyzed his mixed feelings about money, he ultimately concluded that money is simply a system of exchange. He worked through his negative feelings, and over time the Universe provided him a great deal of money for the excellent work that he does.

The power of commitment

Did you ever really notice that things seem to happen once you really and truly make up your mind to have something happen? It's as if the whole Universe just lines up and creates this *thing* for you. It's

When you really want something to happen, the whole universe conspires so that your wish comes true.

—PAULO COELHO

as if the sun, moon and the stars line up and point to the result that you want. This *line up* happens at the time of mental and emotional commitment. It's in a place where we really and truly *know* what *must* happen and that *we will not accept anything less*. At this point of commitment, our minds shift. And, as our minds shift it seems as if the whole Universe shifts as well—for *us*. We almost move into a different dimension or plane as we operate on what we want to have happen. Everything just seems to fall into place and we move ourselves from a place of burden to a place of freedom—a place where we are totally and absolutely clear about what we need and want to have happen and then it does happen.

The key point is getting our minds wrapped around what we really and truly want. This means a commitment that we will not allow any other thing to happen other than what we have just committed ourselves to with the Universe. Now you should be asking

Your vision will become clear only when you look into your heart. Who looks outside, dreams. Who looks inside, awakens.

—CARL GUSTAV JUNG

yourself, "Okay, I agree with all of this, but how do I get myself to this point of commitment? How do I make it all come about in my life? How do I take myself from where I am to where I want to go?" These are all very valid questions. And to them, I respond, listen to the inner *you*—the deepest part of yourself. Go into meditation and talk to yourself about where you are and about where you want to go. Ask yourself how you can best get yourself to commit. Ask yourself how you can get yourself from "here" to "there." The answer lies within *you*. It is not "out there." It is "in here" and the only way for you to find it is to go within and listen.

Listen hard and be honest. Don't dodge what is truth for you. The answers that you seek are inside of you. If you trust your Higher Self and you allow your Higher Self to speak to you, to express to you what *is*, what you need to know, what you need to do, you will find out where you are and where you need to go next. This is a gamble for many people because they truly do not trust themselves—and they do not believe that they have a Higher Self that is really looking out for their greater good.

> *"How do I take myself from where I am to where I want to go?" ... Listen to the inner YOU— the deepest part of yourself. Go into meditation and ask yourself how you can get yourself from "here" to "there." The answer lies within you.*

The importance of meditation and visualization

We have already said that how we perceive things many times is the "reality" for us. If we see something as negative, it's negative to us, and conversely, if we see it as positive, it's positive to us. Our attitudes and our perceptions affect our approach to life. What we put into it is what we get out. I like to use the phrase "Energy begets energy." Once you start something moving it seems to pick up momentum and move itself over time. It's like rolling a ball down a hill. It takes our initial *push* to propel the ball but once it starts moving down the hill, gravity takes over and the ball continues to move on its own.

Listen to the quietest whispers of your mind.
They are telling you the choices
that will help you the most.
—SHAD HELMSTETTER

Many times people ask me how to start the initial push. I find that meditation and visualization work extremely well in getting our dreams, goals and ideas out into the Universe. I find that the best times for meditation is just when you're falling asleep or just as you're waking up. It is in that half-sleep state that helps most people tie into the Universe.

If you believe in God, then share your thoughts with God as you pray just as you're waking up or falling asleep. If you don't believe in God, then think of the Universe and the power of the Universe. Let your subconscious mind work. In the last chapter, I described the "Drain/Gain" exercise. Now that we've discussed your dream, think of your dream—of the desired state that you want—when you are doing the exercise. See yourself there having or doing your dream. Bring it into yourself by pulling it in from the Universe.

There is a company called Centerpointe (www.centerpointe.com) that puts out a series of outstanding meditation CDs that I use myself and I recommend to people for whom I've done life plans. Centerpointe uses "binaural beat auditory technology" to bring the listener into a very deep meditative state. In order for the technology to work, the listener uses a stereo headset and a CD player of some sort. When the CD is played, all that is consciously heard is the sound of rain and of gongs, but actually there are subliminal sounds beneath the surface. Because it is in stereo, a different sound is put into each ear. The sound in the right ear causes a "ping" in the left lobe of the brain and the sound in the left ear causes a "ping" in the right lobe of the brain. The two "pings" cause a neural connection in the brain. As the sound waves deepen, they induce a relaxed state of meditation. Through sound technology the listener is brought from Beta (our natural awake state) to Alpha (relaxation) to Theta (when REM sleep happens) and then Delta, which is the deepest level that we go into. Delta state is where the yogis go when they meditate.

If you are not excited about your own dream, how can you expect anybody else to be?

—LES BROWN

The use of a stereo headset is a must in order for this technology to work; it is useless to just listen without stereo headsets. (The sounds are pleasant but the effect of the meditative state won't be there.) I find that I need to close my eyes, relax and just listen for an hour a day. Centerpointe maintains that by doing this, a person can open themselves more to the abundance and flow of the Universe. Centerpointe aims to help you find your "center point" (the inner core of you). By focusing on your meditation, you can open yourself up to healing, abundance, peace—anything that you want. My clients and I have found the tapes to be extremely effective. There are other companies besides Centerpointe who provide a similar auditory experience—so do some research. By the way, *do not* use these tapes while driving. They really do lull you into a very "floaty" meditative state. As with any product, it is important to follow the directions given to you by the manufacturer.

Dream lofty dreams, and as you dream, so shall you become …
Dreams are the seedlings of reality.

—JAMES ALLEN,
AS A MAN THINKETH

55

Some people's dreams

Dan dreamt about spending more time outdoors with his two children. He dreamt of having a teaching position and of creating a company where he would take people on outdoor adventures. Although not always easy, Dan has indeed created this dream for himself.

Dan's Dream:

Draw Your Dreams Worksheet

★ Think about what you want to have happen. What do you dream about doing?
Think about where you are now, what you are doing, who is around you.
Tie into this your ideas about your talents, your strengths and what you say and
believe about yourself. Draw a picture of your dream. Remember that you must
be in the picture and the Universe honors stick figures! Be sure to use color!
Make this picture as real for yourself as possible.

Mariko is from Japan. She loves to travel to the US and to speak English. She dreams of getting a good job that allows her to travel and to meet people—especially the love of her life. Mariko is actively working with her life plan to make her dreams come true.

Mariko's Dream:

Draw Your Dreams Worksheet

★ Think about what you want to have happen. What do you dream about doing?
Think about where you are now, what you are doing, who is around you.
Tie into this your ideas about your talents, your strengths and what you say and
believe about yourself. Draw a picture of your dream. Remember that you must
be in the picture and the Universe honors stick figures! Be sure to use color!
Make this picture as real for yourself as possible.

Evan dreamt of being an urban planner, where he would build roads and mass transit systems to easily move people from one place to another. He dreamt of designing public parks and cityscapes. His mission in life is to "leave the world a better place in a tangible way." He is now working in Philadelphia and his dream is becoming a reality although it is quickly changing. And when he is ready to act upon it, Evan will draw a new dream and create a new plan.

Evan's Dream:

Draw Your Dreams Worksheet

★ Think about what you want to have happen. What do you dream about doing?
Think about where you are now, what you are doing, who is around you.
Tie into this your ideas about your talents, your strengths and what you say and
believe about yourself. Draw a picture of your dream. Remember that you must
be in the picture and the Universe honors stick figures! Be sure to use color!
Make this picture as real for yourself as possible.

Caroline dreamt of marrying the man of her dreams. She dreamt of combining home life with a career—one in which she is a leader, a world traveler, an artist and a public speaker. Caroline is well on her way to fulfilling her dream. Caroline recently wrote to me saying,

Even though it appears that my drawing was done by a child more than an adult, thank you for including my dreams in your work and more importantly, helping to make my dreams a reality. Your sessions truly gave me such amazing clarity and opened up a space for me to create new dreams. I have recognized the tremendous power of constantly dreaming and feel excited about all of the wonderful opportunities that lie ahead. (I see I conveniently left the bottom right hand side of my drawing with a little space for all the new dreams!)

Caroline's Dream:

Draw Your Dreams Worksheet

★ Think about what you want to have happen. What do you dream about doing? Think about where you are now, what you are doing, who is around you. Tie into this your ideas about your talents, your strengths and what you say and believe about yourself. Draw a picture of your dream. Remember that you must be in the picture and the Universe honors stick figures! Be sure to use color! Make this picture as real for yourself as possible.

Todd dreamt of integrating all aspects of himself to achieve a higher purpose. He wanted to enjoy his family, his community and his career while he received guidance from God / a Higher Power. Recently Todd commented on his drawing and its effect on him. Todd wrote, *"Mary, during the difficult past few years, I pulled out my Life Plan drawing many times to keep me grounded in what matters most to me."* Todd is definitely living his dream, and by reminding his conscious mind of his subconscious desires, he is able to stay focused on achieving them.

Todd's Dream:

Draw Your Dreams Worksheet

★ Think about what you want to have happen. What do you dream about doing?
Think about where you are now, what you are doing, who is around you.
Tie into this your ideas about your talents, your strengths and what you say and
believe about yourself. Draw a picture of your dream. Remember that you must
be in the picture and the Universe honors stick figures! Be sure to use color!
Make this picture as real for yourself as possible.

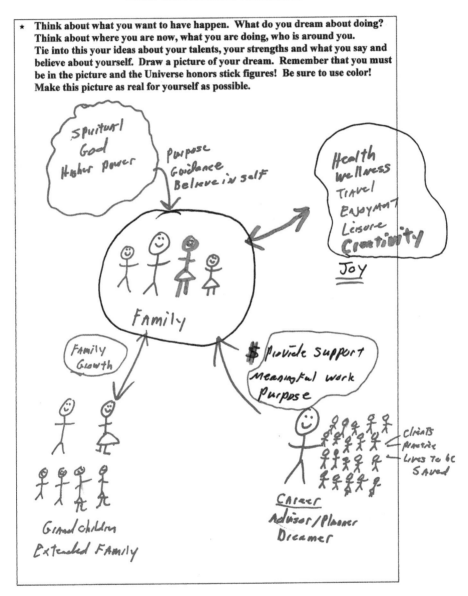

Cathy dreamt of sharing her gifts with others. She dreamt of leaving her job in a high tech company and forming a company of her own. She dreamt of traveling and helping other people transform their own lives. Today, Cathy is transitioning her life. She has formed a business and is getting it launched. She travels with "Habitat for Humanity" to help those in need build their own homes. Cathy is also the Executive Director of Design4Kids, which is an organization that works with talented, under-privileged kids to teach them marketing and project management skills by augmenting their creative design skills. At the time of the printing of this book, Cathy has left the high tech company. She is now re-drawing her dreams and will update her life plan.

Cathy's Dream:

Draw Your Dreams Worksheet

★ Think about what you want to have happen. What do you dream about doing? Think about where you are now, what you are doing, who is around you. Tie into this your ideas about your talents, your strengths and what you say and believe about yourself. Draw a picture of your dream. Remember that <u>you must be in the picture</u> and the Universe honors stick figures! Be sure to use color! Make this picture as real for yourself as possible.

I did a life plan for Joseph when he had just graduated from college. Joseph dreamed of getting a good job with a big company in a city. He dreamed of having his own apartment, of working out (hence the muscles!) and of meeting women. Joseph is indeed living his dream, though he will say that his muscles are not as big as the ones he drew in the picture of himself. He is also working on meeting the French girl of his dreams!

Joseph's Dream:

Draw Your Dreams Worksheet

★ Think about what you want to have happen. What do you dream about doing? Think about where you are now, what you are doing, who is around you. Tie into this your ideas about your talents, your strengths and what you say and believe about yourself. Draw a picture of your dream. Remember that you must be in the picture and the Universe honors stick figures! Be sure to use color! Make this picture as real for yourself as possible.

Several years ago, Karen dreamt of traveling, working with children and writing a children's book. Today, Karen is part of a group of speakers and mentors. By implementing a corporate program around personal and team effectiveness and cultural transformation, Karen has devised a method of achieving the travel component of her dream. She is currently completing a writing course and would like to use it further to build upon what she has achieved. It is interesting where the Universe has taken Karen and how Karen has combined her dreams with what has presented itself to her. Karen recently wrote to me saying, "I guess I work with Big Children (we usually call them adults), but work with the child within!"

Karen's Dream:

Draw Your Dreams Worksheet

★ Think about what you want to have happen. What do you dream about doing?
Think about where you are now, what you are doing, who is around you.
Tie into this your ideas about your talents, your strengths and what you say and
believe about yourself. Draw a picture of your dream. Remember that you must
be in the picture and the Universe honors stick figures! Be sure to use color!
Make this picture as real for yourself as possible.

Sarah is a free spirit. She dreamt of creating a life for herself where she could dress as she pleased at work while combining her music abilities with her enjoyment of design, fashion and yoga. She wanted to live in a city to accomplish all of this. Today Sarah is the associate executive director for a dance performance company in New York City. Although she built her life plan to be a librarian and a yoga teacher, the Universe provided a much better solution to match her career to her talents and her joys in life!

Sarah's Dream:

Draw Your Dreams Worksheet

★ Think about what you want to have happen. What do you dream about doing?
Think about where you are now, what you are doing, who is around you.
Tie into this your ideas about your talents, your strengths and what you say and
believe about yourself. Draw a picture of your dream. Remember that you must
be in the picture and the Universe honors stick figures! Be sure to use color!
Make this picture as real for yourself as possible.

Your dreams really can come true!

Now, go get yourself some colored pens, pencil or markers and draw your dreams. Use colors that you like—colors that make you happy. Sit down in a quiet place. Think about what you want to happen. See yourself in your dream and visualize yourself being there. What do you see? What are you doing? Where are you? Who is there with you? Remember some of the points that were mentioned before. Draw yourself into your dream. You must be a part of it. Have the picture portray what is important to you. If you feel that you aren't an artist, that's okay; the Universe honors rudimentary attempts at drawing. Remember to tie into your dream all of your ideas about your core beliefs, your talents and what makes you happy in life. Also, make sure you use color to make this picture as real as possible to you.

*Cherish your visions
and your dreams
as they are the children
of your soul,
the blueprints of your ultimate
achievements.*

—NAPOLEON HILL

She dreams of being a dancer ...
What is *YOUR* dream?

Key Points

Reminders:

Do	Don't
• Use the "Drain/Gain" exercise to bring your dreams into your reality. • Use meditation to be clear about what you really want by going inside yourself and asking the Higher YOU what you want. • Draw your dreams and allow the right lobe of your brain to create a new reality for you	• When things aren't working out as you want them to, don't blame God or the Universe. Look inside yourself. Hear what you are saying. You might actually be giving the Universe a "mixed message" by wanting one thing but feeling worried or afraid of what you are asking for. • Don't buy in to a belief in "lack." The Universe is very big! It can easily give you what you desire. There is definitely enough to go around for everyone.

Scan the QR Code below to buy these beautiful ballerina photos plus other great items.

DESIGN YOUR OWN DESTINY

CHAPTER FIVE

Evaluate Your Alternatives

Vision without action is a daydream.
Action without vision is a nightmare.

—Japanese proverb

In the last chapter you drew your dreams and you saw examples of other people's dreams. When we dream, many times we are thinking of the long term. We brainstorm with ourselves on what we want the actual end goal—the *end state* or *happy state*—to look like. However, life doesn't always work that way. Most of us have to work our way from where we are to where we ultimately want to go. This might take time and it might require us to think about what kinds of short term goals can lead up to this end state.

Think of it this way. If I'm in New York and I ultimately want to drive to California, I'm going to need to go through Pittsburgh, Pennsylvania, St. Louis, Missouri, and many other cities to get there. My long term goal is California but one of my short term goals is Pittsburgh—then maybe St. Louis. I might change my mind as I'm driving, but it's important for me to remember two things: what my end goal is and what I'm choosing as my first short term goal. As I proceed along, I need to keep checking with myself on two things. First, is my long term goal correct? Have I maybe changed my mind? Second, where am I in relation to my first short term goal? How close am I?

As a principle-centered person, you try to stand apart from the emotion of the situation and from other factors that would act on you, and evaluate the options. Looking at the balanced whole—the work needs, the family needs, the other needs that may be involved, and the possible implications of the various alternatives—you'll try to come up with the best solution, taking all factors into consideration. We are limited but we can push back the borders of our limitations.

—Stephen Covey

When I do life plans for people I have found that when they are at a crossroads in their lives, they might have quite a few options on where to go next or what to do next. Because life might present a variety of options, people sometimes get confused. It is as if they are afraid to take an action because this might lead them in the "wrong" direction. Because of this, I created a Life Choices Assessment Tool to help them determine which way to go is best for them.

There are so many choices that we as people can make with our lives. Recently I was working with a couple named Ron and Rita who were getting ready to retire from their jobs. He had worked for 40 years in construction and she was an elementary school teacher. They faced the question of whether they should sell their home and downsize, stay put, buy or rent a Winnebago and tour the country. They also wondered if they should take up hobbies, volunteer time to worthwhile causes or take on second jobs in their newly-retired financial reality. One of the hardest questions they asked themselves was if they should relocate. All their lives they'd lived in the Northeast US. They'd grown tired of the cold and the snow. Now they are considering going to a warmer climate and for them, this would be a big move. Of course, it does not have to be an "all or nothing" scenario. They could do all of these things or part of them. It was hard for them to choose because they had so many options open to them.

Choices / Options	Goals / Dreams
<ul><li>Sell our home and downsize</li><li>Travel—rent a Winnebago and tour the country</li><li>Take up hobbies</li><li>Volunteer</li><li>Get second jobs</li><li>Relocate and go south to warmer weather</li></ul>	<ul><li>Enjoy a happy healthy retirement in more of a warm climate</li></ul>

Ben Franklin 'T' charts

Many times when we are faced with such difficult life choices, we find it hard to figure out what to do next. I find that people tend to get confused and maybe even get a bit frustrated. In working with Ron and Rita, we assessed each option open to them. We began by creating a Ben Franklin 'T' chart.

This is how a Ben Franklin 'T' chart works. Begin by drawing a 'T' on a piece of paper. Put a "+" on one side and a "-"on the other. Write down all of the positive things about that option on the "+" side. Conversely write down all the negative things about that option on the "-" side. Also list what you don't know about this particular option but that you need to know in order to give yourself all of the facts. Last, write down what your *next steps* are.

Option :___ : _____			
+	**-**	**Need to find out**	**Next Steps**

↑
This is the "T" of the Ben Franklin "T" chart

Using the tool in personal life situations / choices

Ron and Rita assessed each of their options by creating a Ben Franklin 'T' chart. Here is what a Ben Franklin 'T' chart looks like filled out for Ron and Rita's first option:

Option #1: Sell our home and downsize

+	-	Need to find out	Next Steps
We can get a lot out of that house since we bought it so long ago	Our kids might miss the old homestead	How the kids feel about us moving	Talk to the kids
Our house is too big. It is too difficult for Rita to clean. It is time to get rid of the clutter	Where would everyone get together and would they still visit us?	How much could we get for our house and how much would a new one or a condo cost?	Talk to our realtor, Barbara Stout, about our house and its potential sale

Here is what a Ben Franklin 'T' chart looks like filled out for Ron and Rita's second option, which is to travel for an extended period of time.

Option #2: Travel and rent a Winnebago

+	–	Need to find out	Next Steps
We'll finally be able to see the rest of the country	This means a lot of driving for Ron. Rita doesn't feel comfortable driving such a big vehicle	How much would a Winnebago cost?	Find out the cost of a Winnebago for 3-4 months. Maybe we should buy or rent a used one?
We are healthy enough and young enough to take this trip—we need to do it while we can	We'd be leaving our house for a long time and we need to get someone to look after the place	Maybe we would be better off driving a portion of it in a car and then getting a Winnebago in the Midwest somewhere	Find out the options on getting a Winnebago in the Chicago area
	Could be expensive	Who can we get to watch our house while we are gone?	Talk to Ron Jr. about checking on the house while we're gone
	We won't have time for hobbies and volunteer time		

Here is what a Ben Franklin 'T' chart looks like filled out for Ron and Rita's third option:

Option #3: Relocate and go south

+	−	Need to find out	Next Steps
We'd be able to live in warm weather	We will be awfully far from our kids. Will they visit us?	If we go south, where would we go?	Research some places online
If we choose a good retirement community, we can work things out financially if we sell our house for a good price and live modestly	We are getting older. Ron is 68 and Rita is 66. What about healthcare? We will be leaving our established medical care.	The cost of living in various destinations	House hunting trip
		The medical options open to us in other communities	

Here is what a Ben Franklin 'T' chart looks like filled out for Ron and Rita's fourth option:

Option #4: Stay where we are

+	-	Need to find out	Next Steps
We are comfortable in this town—we know everyone	This house and town are expensive—particularly now that we are retiring	How much will it REALLY cost us to stay here?	
We have a great spiritual community here	After 30 years in this house, we would like a change		
Our children & grandchildren view this house as theirs			

Once the Ben Franklin 'T' chart was created, I then asked Ron and Rita, "What is important to *you*? What is important to you intellectually—in the use of your minds? What is important to you physically—in your health? You are both getting older but you are healthy. What else is important to you physically—in your material world? What is important in your home, in your family life, in your lifestyle? What is important to you spiritually? What is important to you emotionally?" I asked them to make a list of these items.

Here are some examples that various people have used in their life plans. I told Ron and Rita that they did not need to use all or any of these. Just list what is important to them in their lives now.

INTELLECTUAL

- Can continue to grow and learn
- Can learn the things that I've always wanted to learn just for the sake of play and not work
- Use my mind less—it's too overactive
- Have a circle of friends to share ideas and experiences with

PHYSICAL —HEALTH

- Be able to stay in balance
- Be where we want to be environmentally and geographically
- Have access to good medical care and medical options
- Pursue recreational activities
- Do more exercise
- Relax more
- Take up hobbies
- Have health benefits

PHYSICAL—WEALTH / MATERIAL WORLD

- Have enough money to be comfortable
- Make a lot of money
- Get a job with the financial compensation that meets my needs
- Spend less time to get the maximum amount of money
- Get benefits
- Pay for schooling
- Financial security

SPIRITUAL

- Integrate my spiritual pursuits with my activities and personal ideas
- Allows me the time I need to meditate regularly
- Meditate
- Journal regularly
- Do yoga to relax my mind and meditate at the same time
- Find a church that aligns with our beliefs
- Attend church or join a spiritual community
- Walk in nature and commune with God
- Find joy in life
- Communicate with God and with Spirit
- Pray

EMOTIONAL

- Is a healthy environment that allows time for my family and friends
- Is good for my marriage
- A situation where all of my family members will benefit
- An environment that is conducive to minimal family disruptions
- An environment that promotes emotional health
- A situation where my needs are met

Ron and Rita's Life Choices worksheet

What is important to you INTELLECTUALLY or from a learning perspective in an opportunity?
▪ No matter what we do, we want to keep our minds in balance—using them to learn but not overusing them to worry and fret ▪ Learn new things ▪ I can learn to paint! I have always wanted to learn to paint with light! (Rita)
What is important to you PHYSICALLY (in your finances / money or health / body) in an opportunity?
▪ Live in a warm climate ▪ Have access to excellent medical care—we are getting older! ▪ Have enough money to live comfortably
What is important to you SPIRITUALLY in an opportunity?
▪ We go to church regularly and we want to make sure that there is a church community locally where we feel "at home"
What is important to you EMOTIONALLY in an opportunity?
▪ We both want to live a peaceful, happy life ▪ We'd like the kids to "buy in" to whatever option we choose

Creating a Life Choices Assessment tool

So far Ron and Rita have created a Ben Franklin 'T' chart for themselves that assesses the potential options that they are facing now. They also have laid out what is important to them in each category: Intellectual, Physical, Spiritual and Emotional. The next step to be done was to score the various options to determine which was the best one for them.

In order to assess the value of something, people normally give it a rating. The score determines the relative good or bad of the thing in question. Of course, everyone has their own sense of what is good or bad for them. That is why a single assessment tool cannot be the same for each person. Each person's life is different as are their values, needs and options. When I do life plans for people, we create an individual Life Choices Assessment tool for each person or couple. This tool is based on what is important to that person/couple along with the score that the person/couple gives a particular item.

In scoring, use the following values:

> **Scoring Criteria**
> 5 = Excellent
> 4 = Very good
> 3 = Good
> 2 = Fair
> 1 = Poor

Once you have scored a particular section, such as Intellectual, average out the numbers to one decimal point and give that section an average score. By doing this, you can see how one option compares to the next for each section.

Ron & Rita's Life Choices Assessment tool

In previous examples, Ron and Rita evaluated what is important to them. They started by scoring their first option, which they called "Option 1", which is to sell their home and downsize.

In Figure 5.1 Ron and Rita assigned "scores" to each of the things that are important to them. They felt that they wanted to open themselves up to adventure—to new and exciting opportunities. They wanted to ensure that they made time for their hobbies and volunteer work. Ron and Rita are pragmatic; they want to live within their means, finding a good community with a church that they can belong to along with good medical care. Lastly, Ron and Rita wanted to make sure that whatever option they choose, they could still be a part of their children's and grandchildren's lives.

After Ron and Rita had scored each criterion, they calculated the average score for each section. Option 1 scored 4.0 in Intellectual, 4.5 in Physical (Health and Wealth), 5.0 in Spiritual and 3.5 in Emotional. Option 1 scored a total of 42 points.

Figure 5.1

Ron & Rita's Life Choices criteria	OPTION 1 Sell home & downsize
INTELLECTUAL	
Exposure to exciting new experiences	4
Availability for hobbies and volunteering	4
Adventure	4
Subtotaled Average	4.0
PHYSICAL (HEALTH AND WEALTH)	
Cost of the option	5
Be where we want to be environmentally & geographically	3
Live within our means	5
Have access to good medical options	5
Subtotaled Average	4.5
SPIRITUAL	
Belong to a like-minded church	5
Subtotaled Average	5.0
EMOTIONAL	
We can visit the kids	5
The kids can visit us	2
Subtotaled Average	3.5
Total Score of All Criteria	42

In Figure 5.2, Ron and Rita compared traveling in a Winnebago (Option 2) with selling their house and downsizing (Option 1). Ron and Rita felt that the Winnebago option was definitely adventuresome but they were concerned mostly with the finances. They also weren't sure about the access to good medical care if the need arose. Ron and Rita scored each item in Option 2 by comparing it to the score they gave that item in Option 1. They asked themselves if the criterion was better, worse or the same as Option 1. After Ron and Rita had scored each criterion, they calculated the average score for each section. Option 2 scored 3.3 in Intellectual. It scored 3.0 in Physical (Health and Wealth). It scored 3.0 in Spiritual. Lastly, it scored 3.0 in Emotional. Option 2 scored a total of 31 points as compared to 42 points in Option 1.

Figure 5.2

Ron & Rita's Life Choices Criteria	OPTION 1 Sell home & downsize	OPTION 2 Travel in a Winnebago
INTELLECTUAL		
Exposure to exciting new experiences	4	4
Availability for hobbies and volunteering	4	1
Adventure	4	5
Subtotaled Average	4.0	3.3
PHYSICAL (HEALTH AND WEALTH)		
Cost of the option	5	3
Be where we want to be environmentally & geographically	3	4
Live within our means	5	3
Have access to good medical options	5	2
Subtotaled Average	4.5	3.0
SPIRITUAL		
Belong to a like-minded church	5	3
Subtotaled Average	5.0	3.0
EMOTIONAL		
We can visit the kids	5	5
The kids can visit us	2	1
Subtotaled Average	3.5	3.0
Total Score of All Criteria	42	31

In Figure 5.3 Ron and Rita assessed Option 3 (moving south) against the two other options presented. This option was very attractive to them and the biggest drawback was their ability to visit with their children and grandchildren. Option 3 scored 4.3 in Intellectual. It scored 4.0 in Physical (Health and Wealth). It scored 4.0 in Spiritual. Lastly, it scored 2.5 in Emotional. Option 3 scored a total of 38 points as compared to 42 points in Option 1 and 31 points in Option 2. In Ron and Rita's minds, Option 3 was very attractive.

Figure 5.3

Ron & Rita's Life Choices Criteria	OPTION 1 Sell home & downsize	OPTION 2 Travel in a Winnebago	OPTION 3 Go south
INTELLECTUAL			
Exposure to exciting new experiences	4	4	4
Availability for hobbies and volunteering	4	1	4
Adventure	4	5	5
Subtotaled Average	4.0	3.3	4.3
PHYSICAL (HEALTH AND WEALTH)			
Cost of the option	5	3	4
Be where we want to be environmentally & geographically	3	4	5
Live within our means	5	3	4
Have access to good medical options	5	2	3
Subtotaled Average	4.5	3.0	4.0
SPIRITUAL			
Belong to a like-minded church	5	3	4
Subtotaled Average	5.0	3.0	4.0
EMOTIONAL			
We can visit the kids	5	5	3
The kids can visit us	2	1	2
Subtotaled Average	3.5	3.0	2.5
Total Score of All Criteria	42	31	38

In Figure 5.4 Ron and Rita assessed Option 4 (staying where they are) against the three other options presented. They considered this option "safe" but it just didn't help them fulfill their need for adventure. Option 4 scored 3.7 in Intellectual. It scored 3.0 in Physical (Health and Wealth). It scored 5.0 in Spiritual. Lastly, it scored 4.5 in Emotional. Option 4 scored a total of 37 points as compared to 42 points in Option 1, 31 points in Option 2 and 38 points in Option 3.

Figure 5.4

Ron & Rita's Life Choices Criteria	OPTION 1 Sell home & downsize	OPTION 2 Travel in a Winnebago	OPTION 3 Go south	OPTION 4 Stay where we are
INTELLECTUAL				
Exposure to exciting new experiences	4	4	4	5
Availability for hobbies and volunteering	4	1	4	4
Adventure	4	5	5	3
Subtotaled Average	4.0	3.3	4.3	3.7
PHYSICAL (HEALTH AND WEALTH)				
Cost of the option	5	3	4	2
Be where we want to be environmentally & geographically	3	4	5	3
Live within our means	5	3	4	2
Have access to good medical options	5	2	3	5
Subtotaled Average	4.5	3.0	4.0	3.0
SPIRITUAL				
Belong to a like-minded church	5	3	4	5
Subtotaled Average	5.0	3.0	4.0	5.0
EMOTIONAL				
We can visit the kids	5	5	3	4
The kids can visit us	2	1	2	5
Subtotaled Average	3.5	3.0	2.5	4.5
Total Score of All Criteria	42	31	38	37

In Figure 5.5 Ron and Rita averaged each criterion for each option. There were 10 criteria in total for their life choices. They added all of them up and divided by 10. Option 1 scored 4.2 on average, which means that in Ron and Rita's opinion this option is between "very good" and "excellent." Option 2 scored 3.1, which is "good" from Ron and Rita's point of view. Option 3 scored 3.8. Option 4 scored 3.7.

Figure 5.5

Ron & Rita's Life Choices Criteria	OPTION 1 Sell home & downsize	OPTION 2 Travel in a Winne-bago	OPTION 3 Go south	OPTION 4 Stay where we are
INTELLECTUAL				
Exposure to exciting new experiences	4	4	4	5
Availability for hobbies and volunteering	4	1	4	4
Adventure	4	5	5	3
Subtotaled Average	4.0	3.3	4.3	3.7
PHYSICAL (HEALTH AND WEALTH)				
Cost of the option	5	3	4	2
Be where we want to be environmentally & geographically	3	4	5	3
Live within our means	5	3	4	2
Have access to good medical options	5	2	3	5
Subtotaled Average	4.5	3.0	4.0	3.0
SPIRITUAL				
Belong to a like-minded church	5	3	4	5
Subtotaled Average	5.0	3.0	4.0	5.0
EMOTIONAL				
We can visit the kids	5	5	3	4
The kids can visit us	2	1	2	5
Subtotaled Average	3.5	3.0	2.5	4.5
Total Score of All Criteria	42	31	38	37
Average of All Criteria	4.2	3.1	3.8	3.7
RANKED OPTIONS	1	4	2	3

I'm sure that you're wondering what Ron and Rita chose to do in the end. They chose to sell their house and take an extended trip by car around the US. When the next winter came, they rented a modest house in the South for three months so that they would miss the worst of the cold weather. Because they chose an area that was a two-hour drive to various attractions, their children and grandchildren came to visit them during the winter school vacation week. Ron and Rita combined their various options and came up with the option that worked best for them!

Robert and Jessica's Ben Franklin 'T' charts

I also worked with another couple named Robert and Jessica who really wanted a child. They had been trying for a few years with no success. Their questions at this point in their lives were:

- Should we go to a fertility clinic?
- Should we remain childless?
- Should we adopt?
- Should we change our expectations?
- Should we just continue to let nature take its course?

Robert and Jessica assessed each of these options by creating a Ben Franklin 'T' chart. Here is what a Ben Franklin 'T' chart looks like filled out for Robert and Jessica's first option:

Option #1: Go to a fertility clinic

+	-	Need to find out	Next Steps
We've tried everything else	It can be painful	Options on what's available and at what cost	Talk to the Jefferson's about their experience with this
Technology has improved. It might work	Expensive		

Here is what a Ben Franklin 'T' chart looks like filled out for Robert and Jessica's second option:

Option #2: Remain childless

+	-	Need to find out	Next Steps
This is what we have now	We both really want a child		
More time for other activities and travel	Emotionally Jessica feels that someone is missing in our lives		

Here is what a Ben Franklin 'T' chart looks like filled out for Robert and Jessica's third option:

Option #3: Adopt a child

+	−	Need to find out	Next Steps
We will have a child to love and care for	Robert knows that he will love the child but he really wants to continue trying to have our own child.	Find out how hard it is to get a baby from the U.S.	Jessica will call around to U.S. adoption agencies
We won't need to go through the emotional trauma of the fertility clinic	It's still not a sure thing if we'll get a baby. Healthy U.S. babies are hard to get. Maybe we should try for a baby from another country.	Find out about babies from outside the U.S.	Jessica will also talk with Peggy Johnson about her baby girl from Asia; Jessica will get the agency information details from Peggy as well.
		Expensive—legal fees, travel, medical expenses	Costs, timeframe, availability of babies
		Might be a long waiting period	Will we know the child's genetics / potential health problems?

Here is what a Ben Franklin 'T' chart looks like filled out for Robert and Jessica's fourth option:

Option #4: Change our expectations

+	-	Need to find out	Next Steps
It might make it easier for us to accept where we are right now	It will be hard to change our expectations if our hearts' desire is a child	How would we change our expectations?	Go to counseling? Find out each other's true feelings on this matter
By changing our expectations, we might be able to open ourselves to other options		Do we really know each other's feelings on this matter?	Maybe make a list of all of the reasons why it would be okay for us to remain childless

Lastly, here's what a Ben Franklin 'T' chart looks like filled out for Robert and Jessica's fifth option:

Option #5: Continue to let nature take its course

+	-	Need to find out	Next Steps
Less expensive	Risky—time is marching on and we've been trying for 5 years with no luck		
It's fun to try!			

Robert and Jessica's Life Choices worksheet

What is important to you INTELLECTUALLY or from a learning perspective in an opportunity?
▪ We will definitely learn new things no matter which way we go—but there's nothing intellectual about this option for us!
What is important to you PHYSICALLY (in your finances / money or health / body) in an opportunity?
▪ We prefer to always live within our means though if we need to pay to have a child, we will do it, depending on the cost ▪ We do not know the toll that a fertility clinic will have on Jessica's body.
What is important to you SPIRITUALLY in an opportunity?
▪ We both believe in God. We do not go to church regularly but we are very spiritual. Jessica believes that someone is missing from our lives.
What is important to you EMOTIONALLY in an opportunity?
▪ We both want a child so badly. ▪ We have gotten used to our time freedom and we know that having a child will radically change our lifestyle.

As Robert and Jessica so clearly state, there was nothing intellectual about this decision for them. Therefore in Figure 5.6, you will see scores of 0 in the Intellectual category for the evaluation of each option.

Robert and Jessica's Life Choices Assessment tool

Figure 5.6

Robert & Jessica's Life Choices Criteria	OPTION 1 Fertility clinic	OPTION 2 Remain childless	OPTION 3 Adopt	OPTION 4 Change our expecta-tions	OPTION 5 Let nature take its course
INTELLECTUAL	0	0	0	0	0
Subtotaled Average	0.0	0.0	0.0	0.0	0.0
PHYSICAL (HEALTH AND WEALTH)					
Expense	1	5	1	4	5
Potential success rate	5	1	4	1	1
Known genetics of the child in terms of health	5	1	2	2	5
Time freedom	2	5	2	5	3
Subtotaled Average	3.3	3.0	2.3	3.0	3.5
SPIRITUAL					
Feeling abundant and "whole" as a family	5	1	4	3	2
Feels natural	1	2	2	4	5
Subtotaled Average	3.0	1.5	3.0	3.5	3.5
EMOTIONAL					
Feeling of loss of not having a child	4	1	4	3	2
Emotional expense	5	1	4	4	2
Subtotaled Average	4.5	1.0	4.0	3.5	2.0
Total Score of All Criteria	28	17	23	26	25
Average of All Criteria	3.5	2.1	2.9	3.3	3.1
RANKED OPTIONS	1	5	4	2	3

As you can see in Figure 5.6, Robert and Jessica's top ranked choice is to go to a fertility clinic. They are aware that it will be expensive but they are also aware that adopting (which comes in as their fourth ranked choice) is also expensive. Although changing their expectations is an option, they just could not go with that one. Their hearts "overrode" that option because they both felt a loss of not having a child.

Robert and Jessica went to the fertility clinic. Jessica conceived twins. It was a difficult pregnancy because Jessica was bed-ridden or had to stay on the couch during most of her pregnancy. But Robert and Jessica both say it was worth the cost—especially when they look into the eyes of their son and daughter!

Using the tool in career and business choices

The last two plans that I showed you (Ron & Rita and Robert & Jessica) demonstrated that you can use this tool in your every day life. But when you are evaluating a job change, some of the charts change slightly. Let's go into John Jennings' options for his life, since so many of the choices were about work and his job. John and I created a Ben Franklin 'T' chart for each of his options.

John's options were:

1) To stay with his current job and go to night school to finish his degree

2) To change companies to obtain a "bigger job" with more money, or

3) To quit his job, take a loan and write his book

Option #1: Stay with my current job and go to night school to finish my degree

+	-	Need to find out	Next Steps
I can make money while I finish my degree	It might take me a long time to get through night school	What will it take to be accepted in an accelerated degree program?	Talk to Hesser College about their night school program
My company will actually "chip in" and pay for part of my degree	Part of me wants to "go for broke" and tackle the risk and write the book now	How much will my company pay? Find out if all classes "count"— like creative writing courses	Talk to Judi Brown in HR about my company's benefits
I know my current job. I can go after a promotion and make more money—this won't take away from night school			

Here is what a Ben Franklin 'T' chart looks like filled out for John's second option, which is to go with Harkins Technology and take on a new job. This job has increased responsibility, pressure and travel. It also pays more than what John is making now.

Option #2: Change companies to a "bigger" job with more money

+	-	Need to find out	Next Steps
Harkins Technology wants to hire me to a bigger job that pays more money	Huge ramp up time to get "up to speed" on the job	Find out more about the Harkins job. Find out if I'm jumping from the "frying pan into the fire"	Talk to Jim Lester at Harkins and find out more about this job and what they are looking for
We can save up more money for college for the kids and also for my degree in the future	Less time with Michele and the kids		
	Increased stress		
	More travel		

Here is what a Ben Franklin 'T' chart looks like filled out for John's third option, which is to quit his job, take out a loan against his house and write his book. This option was extremely risky in John's mind, but part of him wanted to take this risk.

Option #3: Quit my job, take a loan and write my book

+	**-**	**Need to find out**	**Next Steps**
I can do what I've always dreamed of doing—be a writer	Extremely risky	Find an agent and test out my book concept	Ask around about a book agent
For the first time in my life, I can live my dream	Not sure if my book is really "marketable"	Talk to Michele and find out how she REALLY feels about this	Create the materials to send to the agent
	I'm a little afraid. What if I fail? Or what if it takes too long and we run out of money?	Is it realistic to get an advance?	Estimate how long it would take me to finish the book if I was to write full time

Once the Ben Franklin 'T' chart was created, I asked John to think about what was important to him in the Professional/Career/Job aspect of his life? What was important to him in the Aesthetics/Lifestyle realm of his life? What was important in his home or his family life? How about his material world? What about what was important to him in the Financial/Money aspect of his life? I asked him to make a list of these items. (Please note that when I use the term "Aesthetics/Lifestyle" by this I mean what is important to people in how their lives are lived; these are usually very personal choices/preferences of things that are viewed as beautiful, pleasurable, advantageous, desirable or valuable. Examples of Aesthetics/Lifestyle choices are throughout the remaining examples in this chapter.)

When you make a list of the items that are important to you, take into consideration your needs in keeping your life in balance. Consider your

Intellectual, Physical, Spiritual and Emotional needs. Make sure that your values are reflected in the things that you list as important to you.

Here are some examples that various people have used in their life plans. You do not need to use any or all of these. Just list what is important to you in your life—for any choice that you are making at this stage in your life.

FINANCIAL / MONEY

- Make a lot of money
- Make money to live comfortably
- Spend less time to get the maximum amount of money
- Get a job that is predictable financially
- Get a job that has room for financial growth
- Get benefits
- Pay for schooling
- Can grow to financial freedom
- Financial security
- Can help me pay off school loans

AESTHETICS / LIFESTYLE

- Be able to stay in balance
- Be where I want to be environmentally and geographically
- Involve my daughter in my business
- Be creative
- Minimize hassles
- Integrate my spiritual pursuits with my activities and personal ideas
- Freedom
- Impact on my marriage
- Impact on my family
- Impact on my volunteer activities
- Aligns with my goals
- Ensures my needs are met
- Is flexible enough to deal with compromises
- Allows time with my family
- Work from home if desired
- Aligns with my goals
- Time for social pursuits
- Vacation time
- Travel required

PROFESSIONAL / CAREER / JOB

- Non-corporate
- Is one of the top companies worldwide
- Can leverage my professional skills
- Ability to learn
- Creativity in job
- Variety
- Recognition potential
- Allows me to be a supervisor
- Has minimal supervision
- Has work flow freedom
- Allows me to be effective
- Gives me a competitive advantage
- Allows me leadership potential
- Intellectually challenging
- Prestigious
- Has variety
- Allows me to manage my public and private interests
- Flexible job
- Good schedule
- Room for career growth
- Fun job
- Interaction with people—team work
- Tackling issues
- Allows me to use my degree
- Steady job
- Opportunity to work alone but within a structured environment
- Wardrobe flexibility

Because changing work is specific to a job situation, I have found that by changing the templates slightly, I was better able to hit the mark for my client's life plans. John Jennings' Life Choices worksheet below is an example of the Life Choices Worksheet for a Job/Career Change. This tool helps people to clarify what is important to them when changing their job or career.

John Jennings' Life Choices worksheet

What is important to you FINANCIALLY or from a MONEY perspective in an opportunity?
<ul><li>Make more money</li><li>Can grow to financial freedom</li><li>Reasonable risk</li><li>Save money for school for kids & me</li></ul>
What is important to you AESTHETICALLY or in your LIFESTYLE in an opportunity?
<ul><li>Spend time with Michele and kids</li><li>Be where I want to be environmentally & geographically</li><li>Vacation time</li><li>Be creative</li><li>Aligns with my goals</li></ul>
What is important to you PROFESSIONALLY—in your CAREER—or in your JOB in an opportunity?
<ul><li>Reasonable travel</li><li>Flexible job</li><li>Good schedule</li><li>Room for career growth</li><li>Fun job</li><li>Using my skills</li><li>Interaction with people</li><li>Keep learning</li></ul>

John Jennings' Life Choices assessment tool

In his Life Choices worksheet, John evaluated what is important to him and his family. He filled out the criteria that matters to him financially, aesthetically and professionally.

In Figure 5.7, John started by scoring his current situation, which he called "Option 1", which was that he could stay in his current job, vie for a promotion and attend night school to finish his degree. His company was willing to help him pay for the schooling. John assigned scores to each of the things that were important to him. He felt that his current job could give him more money with very limited risk. He felt that as he was working at his job, he could attend night school and build up the skills that he needed to be a professional writer. He also felt that his current job situation allowed him to spend time with his wife, Michele and their children. After John had scored each criterion, he calculated the average score for each section and Option 1 scored a total of 66 points.

> *Nothing can add more*
> *power to your life than*
> *concentrating all your energies*
> *on a limited set of targets.*
>
> —Nido Qubein

Figure 5.7

John Jennings' Life Choices criteria	OPTION 1 Current job & night school
FINANCIAL / MONEY	
Make more money	4
Can grow to financial freedom	3
Reasonable risk	3
Save money for school for kids & me	4
Subtotaled Average	3.5
AESTHETICS / LIFESTYLE	
Spend time with Michele & kids	3
Be where I want to be—environmentally & geographically	3
Vacation time	3
Able to live with the pressure	5
Be creative	3
Aligns with my goals	4
Subtotaled Average	3.5
PROFESSIONAL / CAREER / JOB	
Reasonable travel	3
Flexible job	4
Good schedule	3
Room for career growth	4
Fun job	4
Using my skills	4
Interaction with people	4
Keep learning	5
Subtotaled Average	3.9
Total Score of All Criteria	66

In Figure 5.8 John compared the potential new job at Harkins Technology (Option 2) with his current job and night school potential (Option 1). John felt that the new job at Harkins Technology would definitely give him more money with a minimal amount of risk. However, he would be spending very little time with his family as he ramped up into the demands of this new job. His ability to spend time writing or to have vacation time with his family would be severely impacted. He *would* learn, but his life would belong to the company until he became comfortable with the new job and its demands. John scored each item in Option 2 by comparing it to the score he gave that item in Option 1. He asked himself if the criterion was better, worse or the same as Option 1. After John had scored each criterion, he calculated the average score for each section. Option 2 scored 4.5 in Financial/Money. He would definitely make more money in Option 2. However it scored 2.3 in Aesthetics/Lifestyle. In order to get that money, he would have to sacrifice his personal time, his writing time and the time with his family. Lastly, it scored 3.1 in Professional/Career/Job. Option 2 scored a total of 57 points as compared to 66 points in Option 1.

Figure 5.8

John Jennings' Life Choices criteria	OPTION 1 Current job & night school	OPTION 2 New job with more demands
FINANCIAL / MONEY		
Make more money	4	5
Can grow to financial freedom	3	5
Reasonable risk	3	3
Save money for school for kids & me	4	5
Subtotaled Average	3.5	4.5
AESTHETICS / LIFESTYLE		
Spend time with Michele & kids	3	1
Be where I want to be—environmentally & geographically	3	2
Vacation time	3	2
Able to live with the pressure	5	3
Be creative	3	4
Aligns with my goals	4	2
Subtotaled Average	3.5	2.3
PROFESSIONAL / CAREER / JOB		
Reasonable travel	3	1
Flexible job	4	2
Good schedule	3	1
Room for career growth	4	5
Fun job	4	3
Using my skills	4	4
Interaction with people	4	5
Keep learning	5	4
Subtotaled Average	3.9	3.1
Total Score of All Criteria	66	57

In Figure 5.9 John assessed Option 3 (quitting his job, taking a loan and writing his book) against the two other options presented. He rated Option 3 as being very high in risk. He was unsure as to whether he could really live with the pressure of having to write the book and get it published and make money before the money from his loan ran out. Although he wanted this option so much in his heart, his head and his stomach told him that it was a bad choice. Option 3 scored 1.8 in Financial/Money. In John's mind, Option 3 was a huge risk. It scored 3.3 in Aesthetics/Lifestyle. In order to get that money, he would have to sacrifice his personal time, his writing time and the time with his family. Lastly, Option 3 scored 4.0 in Professional/Career/Job. Option 3 scored a total of 59 points. It ranked behind Option 1 by quite a bit but was only ahead of Option 2 by 2 points.

Figure 5.9

John Jennings' Life Choices criteria	OPTION 1 Current job & night school	OPTION 2 New job with more demands	OPTION 3 Quit job / take loan / write book
FINANCIAL / MONEY			
Make more money	4	5	1
Can grow to financial freedom	3	5	4
Reasonable risk	3	3	1
Save money for school for kids & me	4	5	1
Subtotaled Average	3.5	4.5	1.8
AESTHETICS / LIFESTYLE			
Spend time with Michele & kids	3	1	2
Be where I want to be	3	2	4
Vacation time	3	2	3
Able to live with the pressure	5	3	1
Be creative	3	4	5
Aligns with my goals	4	2	5
Subtotaled Average	3.5	2.3	3.3
PROFESSIONAL / CAREER / JOB			
Reasonable travel	3	1	3
Flexible job	4	2	5
Good schedule	3	1	5
Room for career growth	4	5	2
Fun job	4	3	5
Using my skills	4	4	5
Interaction with people	4	5	2
Keep learning	5	4	5
Subtotaled Average	3.9	3.1	4.0
Total Score of All Criteria	66	57	59

In Figure 5.10 John averaged each criterion for each option. There were 18 criteria in total for John's life choices. He added all of them up and divided by 18. Option 1 scored 3.7 on average, which means that in John's opinion this option was between "good" and "very good." Option 2 scored 3.2, which was "good" from John's point of view. Option 3 scored 3.3.

Figure 5.10

John Jennings' Life Choices criteria	OPTION 1 Current job & night school	OPTION 2 New job with more demands	OPTION 3 Quit job / take loan / write book
FINANCIAL / MONEY			
Make more money	4	5	1
Can grow to financial freedom	3	5	4
Reasonable risk	3	3	1
Save money for school for kids & me	4	5	1
Subtotaled Average	3.5	4.5	1.8
AESTHETICS / LIFESTYLE			
Spend time with Michele & kids	3	1	2
Be where I want to be	3	2	4
Vacation time	3	2	3
Able to live with the pressure	5	3	1
Be creative	3	4	5
Aligns with my goals	4	2	5
Subtotaled Average	3.5	2.3	3.3
PROFESSIONAL / CAREER / JOB			
Reasonable travel	3	1	3
Flexible job	4	2	5
Good schedule	3	1	5
Room for career growth	4	5	2
Fun job	4	3	5
Using my skills	4	4	5
Interaction with people	4	5	2
Keep learning	5	4	5
Subtotaled Average	3.9	3.1	4.0
Total Score of All Criteria	66	57	59
Average of all Criteria	3.7	3.2	3.3
RANKED OPTIONS	1	3	2

The tool in Figures 5.7 - 5.10 was created in Microsoft Excel. It uses basic formulas to assess the criteria input into the tool. In this tool, a straight average was used. What this means is that each criteria was *weighted* equally. In John Jennings' example, "using my skills" is just as important as "fun job" or "spend time with Michele and kids" or "reasonable risk." From a *weighted option* point of view, however, the Excel tool could be built so that any criteria could be *weighted more* than another—meaning that it could count more if desired. For the sake of simplicity, I have gone with an equal measure for each criterion. If you want a simple way to weigh a criterion more, put it down twice in a section. For instance, if "reasonable risk" was highly important to John, he could list it twice. Notice in Figure 5.11 how this weighting actually affects the score. Now Option 2 and Option 3 are equal. Just changing this one criterion to "weigh" more heavily than the others changed the values of the final scores. This having been said, it is important that if you are setting this up with equal weighting, list out the key criteria that are important to you—and leave out the things that do not mean a lot to you. Alternatively, you can use a weighted tool but that will require a little forethought from you as you set it up. Always go back to your *gut* to determine the validity of each score and each final result!

Figure 5.11

John Jennings' Life Choices criteria	OPTION 1 Current job & night school	OPTION 2 New job with more demands	OPTION 3 Quit job / take loan / write book
FINANCIAL / MONEY			
Make more money	4	5	1
Can grow to financial freedom	3	5	4
Reasonable risk	3	3	1
Reasonable risk	3	3	1
Save money for school for kids & me	4	5	1
Subtotaled Average	3.4	4.2	1.6
AESTHETICS / LIFESTYLE			
Spend time with Michele & kids	3	1	2
Be where I want to be	3	2	4
Vacation time	3	2	3
Able to live with the pressure	5	3	1
Be creative	3	4	5
Aligns with my goals	4	2	5
Subtotaled Average	3.5	2.3	3.3
PROFESSIONAL / CAREER / JOB			
Reasonable travel	3	1	3
Flexible job	4	2	5
Good schedule	3	1	5
Room for career growth	4	5	2
Fun job	4	3	5
Using my skills	4	4	5
Interaction with people	4	5	2
Keep learning	5	4	5
Subtotaled Average	3.9	3.1	4.0
Total Score of all criteria	69	60	60
Average of all Criteria	3.6	3.2	3.3
RANKED OPTIONS	1	2 or 3	2 or 3

> *It is important that if you are setting this up with equal weighting, list out the key criteria that are important to you—and leave out the things that do not mean a lot to you… Always go back to your gut to determine the validity of each score and each final result! Your gut will lead you to the right option for YOU!*

Key Points

Reminders:

Do	Don't
▪ Look at the options available to you and use the Ben Franklin 'T' chart approach to evaluate the positive and negative aspects of the option. Also determine "what else you need to know" as well as your "next steps."	▪ Don't make the mistake of putting criteria into the Life Choices Assessment tool that are not really important to you. You could skew your results.
▪ Use the **Life Choices Assessment Tool** to quantify the best option for you. This tool helps to put into numbers all of the things that are important to you for each option that you assess.	▪ Don't forget that each criterion might not be equally valuable to you. Because of this, you might want to utilize the weighted averaging approach used in Figure 5.11 as a way to determine the best option for you.!
▪ Always rely on your gut to determine the validity of each score you assign and each final score as it is tallied. Your gut will lead you to the right option for YOU!	

CHAPTER SIX:

Create a Life Choice Map

Take the first step in faith.
You don't have to see the whole staircase. Just take the first step.

—MARTIN LUTHER KING

So far we've discussed how to stay in balance, the alignment of one's talents with one's joys in life, the power of "I AM" statements, the drawing of one's dreams and how to choose which life choice option is best for you. Now we're going to discuss how to map *where you are* to *where you want to go*.

How to create a Life Choice Map

It is really important to create a life choice map when you are deciding how to get *there* from *here*. Again, if you were driving your car from New York to Los Angeles, in all likelihood you would get a series of maps to decide the best route for you to take. The same holds true with your life plan. Question: How do you eat an elephant? Answer: One bite at a time. The more complex your life plan and what you want to accomplish, the more you need a life choice map.

Let's talk through the process of creating a map of your life choices. An example of this process will be provided at the end of this section for you to use to think through your own map.

Step One—Create an Activities List

First ask yourself what life choice option you want to map. Now, take this option and list out what things or actions need to happen in order for this goal to happen. These activities do not need to be in order. Just brainstorm them. You might want to include an activity called "Stay in Balance" since you created a list of "Balance Activities" in Chapter 1.

Begin with the end in mind.

—STEPHEN COVEY

Create an Activities List
What life choice option do you want to map?
▪ List the life choice option that is your dream
Take this option and list out what things or activities need to happen in order for this goal to happen. These activities do not need to be in order. Just brainstorm and list them here.
▪ An Activity ▪ A Different Activity ▪ Another Activity ▪ Still Another Activity ▪ Yet Another Activity ▪ A Totally Different Activity ▪ Some Other Activity

Step Two—Sequence your Activities List

Now sequence these activities so that they lead from your current situation to your new desired situation. What needs to happen first? What needs to happen second, third, etc.? Make sure that everything that *needs* to happen appears in your list. These sequenced activities can now be charted on a map that leads from your current situation to your desired situation.

Step Three—Place your Sequenced Activities on the Life Choice Map

Figure 6.1 depicts that these activities should be placed on the left side of the arrow on the Life Choice Map that you have prepared for yourself. As you draw your own map, be sure to give yourself room from one activity to the next so that the map is spread out. Make sure that everything that needs to happen appears in this map.

If you go to work on your goals,
your goals will go to work on you.
If you go to work on your plan,
your plan will go to work on you.
Whatever good things we build
end up building us.

—JIM ROHN

Figure 6.1

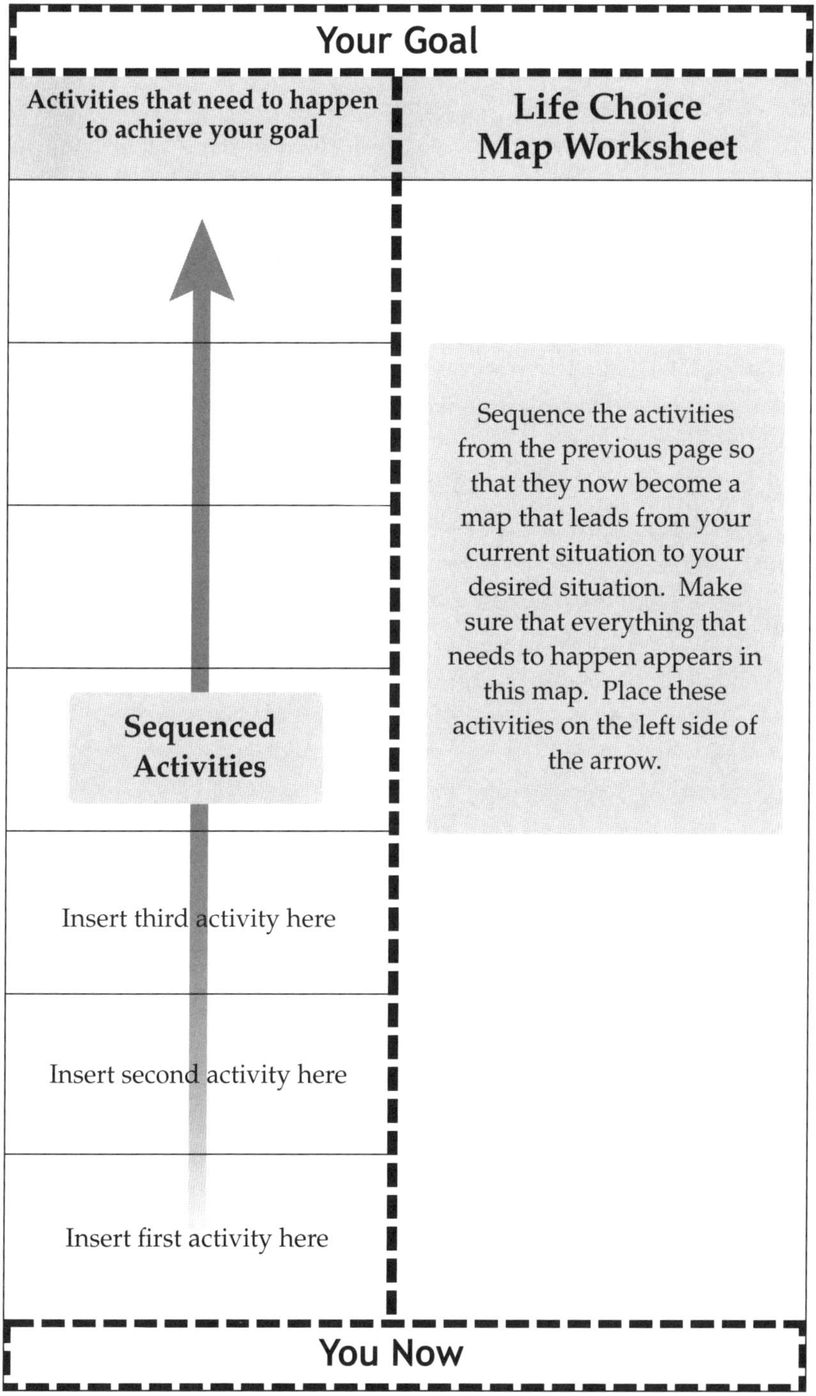
Your Goal
Activities that need to happen to achieve your goal
Life Choice Map Worksheet
Sequenced Activities
Sequence the activities from the previous page so that they now become a map that leads from your current situation to your desired situation. Make sure that everything that needs to happen appears in this map. Place these activities on the left side of the arrow.
Insert third activity here
Insert second activity here
Insert first activity here
You Now

Step Four—Determine the Actions Needed and Your Support People
Figure 6.2 depicts that the actions (that need to be done complete the activity on the left side of the arrow) should be placed on the corresponding position on the right side of the arrow. These actions, when taken, will actually achieve the activity in question.

Be sure to determine who needs to do what in order for that action to be completed. Any plan is only as good as its execution and the people that help to make it happen. Most life plans need more than just *you* to make them happen. They take others who will provide emotional support, guidance, advice or actions that need to be done on your behalf. You need to determine *who* needs to do *what* in order for your plan to work. List all of the things that you need to do as well as the actions of the people who you need help from on the right side of the arrow in the next chart.

You give but little when you
give of your possessions.
It is when you give of yourself
that you truly give.

—Kahlil Gibran

Figure 6.2

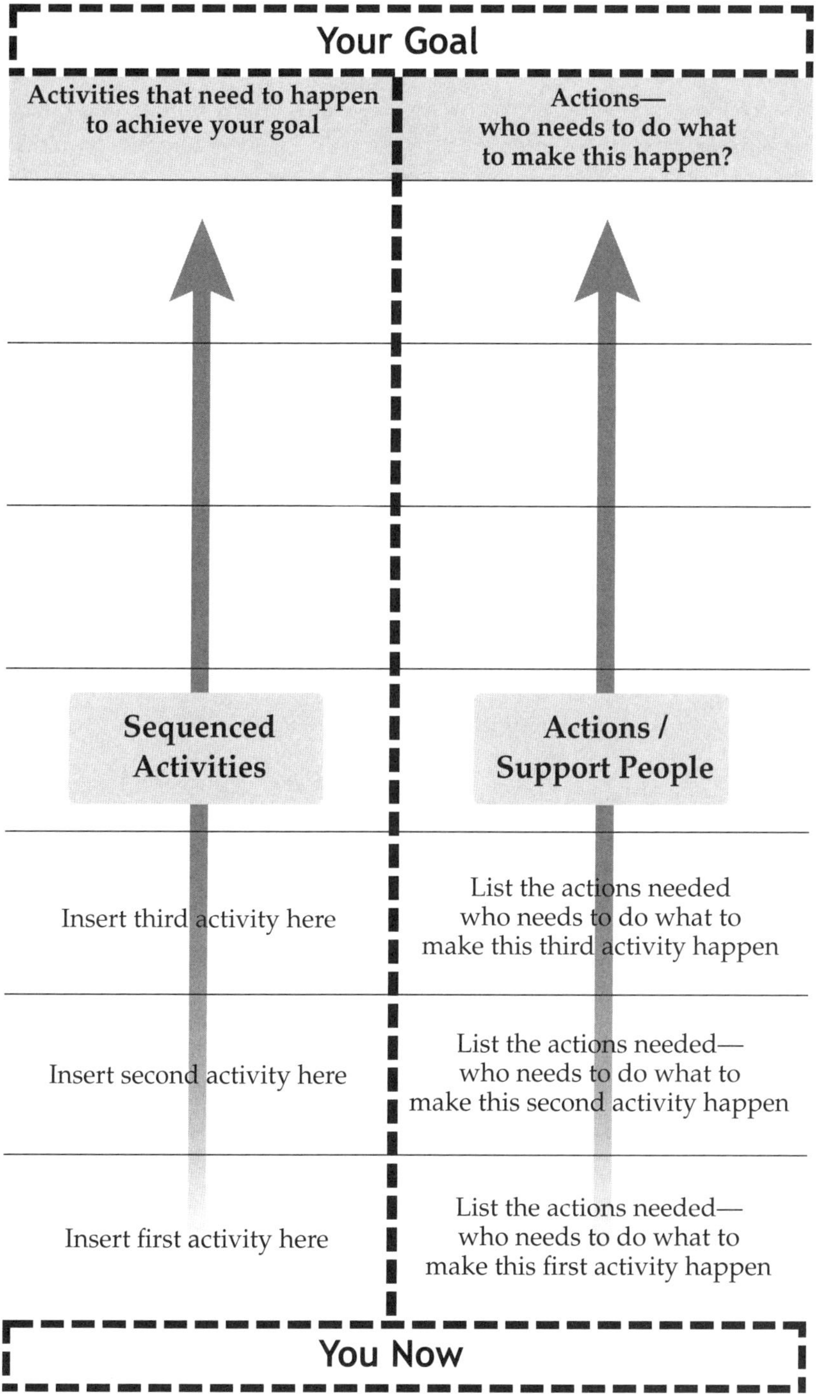

Your Goal	
Activities that need to happen to achieve your goal	**Actions— who needs to do what to make this happen?**
Sequenced Activities	**Actions / Support People**
Insert third activity here	List the actions needed who needs to do what to make this third activity happen
Insert second activity here	List the actions needed— who needs to do what to make this second activity happen
Insert first activity here	List the actions needed— who needs to do what to make this first activity happen
You Now	

Step Five—Determine the Timeframe

Figure 6.3 depicts that the length of time and "due dates" for each of the various actions required should be included in the Life Choice map. These assignments of time should be placed underneath the action that is required to be taken by you or by someone else. Allow time for slippage. Remember that life doesn't always work on your time schedule so allow some leeway in your plan's timing. Think about how long it will take you to complete one action to the next.

The way I see it, there are two kinds of dreams.
One is a dream that's always going to be just that ...
A dream. A vision that you can never really hold
in your hand.
Then there's a dream that's more than a dream it's like
... a map. A map that you live by and follow for the rest
of your days. Knowing that someday you're going
to stand on top of that Mountain holding everything
you thought of.
Right There in Your Hand!

—ROBERT COOPER

Figure 6.3

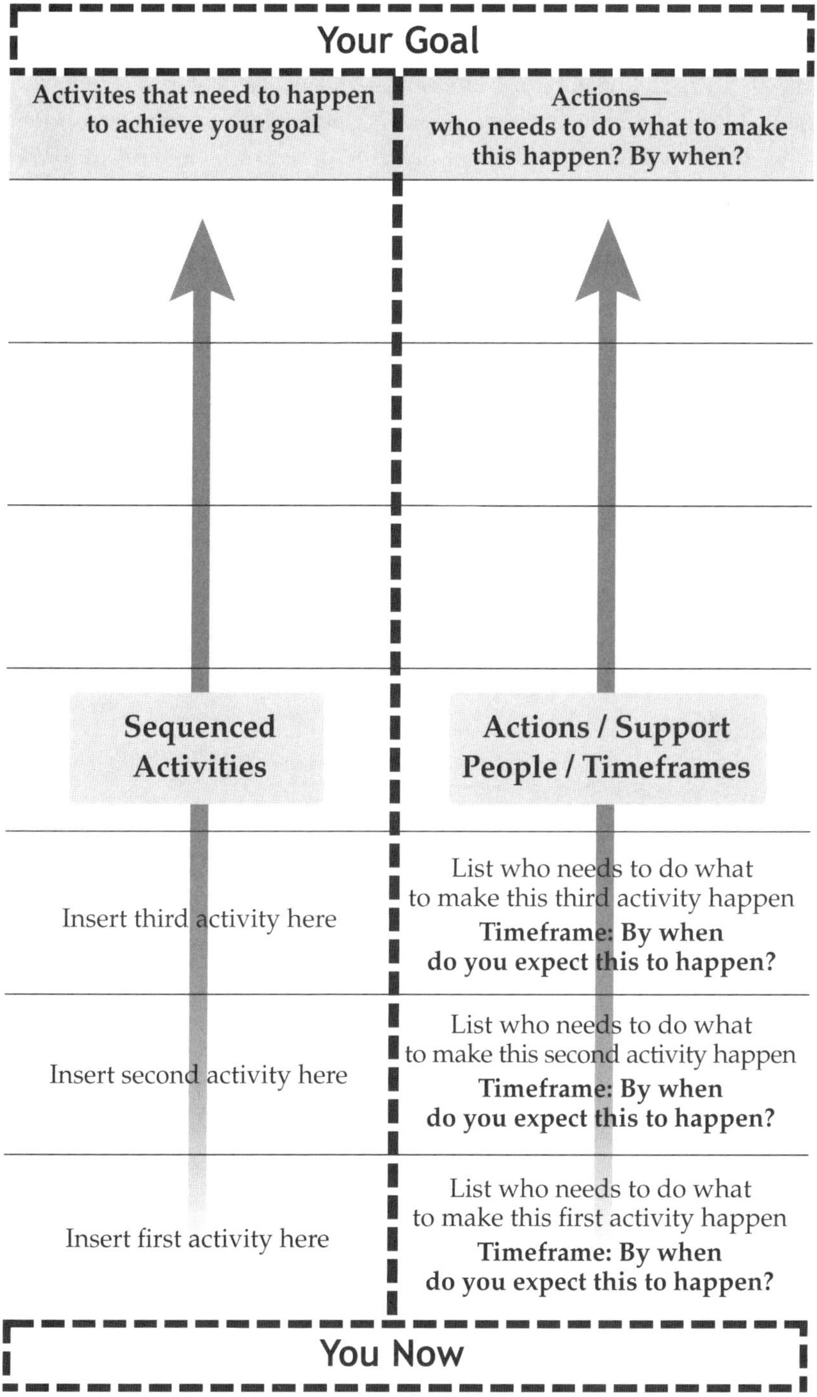

Your Goal

Activites that need to happen to achieve your goal	Actions— who needs to do what to make this happen? By when?

Sequenced Activities

Actions / Support People / Timeframes

Insert third activity here	List who needs to do what to make this third activity happen **Timeframe: By when do you expect this to happen?**
Insert second activity here	List who needs to do what to make this second activity happen **Timeframe: By when do you expect this to happen?**
Insert first activity here	List who needs to do what to make this first activity happen **Timeframe: By when do you expect this to happen?**

You Now

Robin's Life Choice Map

Robin's dream was to be a veterinary assistant. She had quite a few challenges to deal with as she made this dream a reality. First, she was in bad financial straits. She had to secure housing as well as determine how she could finance going to school. Second, Robin had very few computer skills. In today's world, knowing how to use a computer and navigate the internet is a requirement to get through school, so she had to make herself computer literate. She was advised that most schools do have computers available in the library for students to share so her main concern was not access to a computer but how to actually operate it efficiently. Here is Robin's Life Choice's activities list.

If you don't know where you're going,
you just might end up somewhere else.

—Yogi Berra

Step One—Create an Activities List

Robin listed out what things or activities need to happen in order for her goal to become a reality.

Create an Activities List
List all of the things or activities that need to happen in order for your dream to come true. They do not need to be in order. Brainstorm the possibilities.
<ul><li>Learn to use the computer better</li><li>Find an apartment</li><li>Stay in balance</li><li>Move into my new apartment</li><li>Check out local vet assistant schools</li><li>Apply to vet assistant schools and get accepted</li><li>Get my previous school records</li><li>Apply for financial aid/grant</li></ul>

Step Two—Sequence your Activities List

She sequenced these activities so that they now lead from her current situation to her desired situation of being a veterinary assistant.

Create an Activities List
Sequence the above list. Be sure to include all of the things or activities that need to happen in order for your dream to come true.
<ul><li>Stay in balance</li><li>Get my previous school records</li><li>Find an apartment</li><li>Learn to use the computer better</li><li>Check out local vet assistant schools</li><li>Move into my new apartment</li><li>Apply for financial aid/grant</li><li>Apply to vet assistant schools and get accepted</li></ul>

Step Three—Place your Sequenced Activities on the Life Choice Map
In Figure 6.4 Robin placed these sequenced activities on a map that leads from Robin's current situation to her dream of being a veterinary assistant. Please remember that Robin's first needed activity was placed at the bottom of the page and the remaining activities were placed sequentially up the page ending with Robin's final goal.

Developing the plan is actually
laying out the sequence of events
that have to occur for you to
achieve your goal.

—GEORGE L. MORRISEY

Figure 6.4

Robin's Goal	
Activities that need to happen to achieve your goal	**Life Choice Map Worksheet**
Apply to vet assistant schools and get accepted	
Apply for financial aid/grant	
Move into my new apartment	
Check out local vet asst. schools	
Learn to use the computer better	
Find an apartment	
Get my previous school records	
Stay in balance	
Robin Now	

Step Four—Determine the Actions Needed and Your Support People
In Figure 6.5 Robin listed all of the actions that she and others needed to do as well as all of the people of whom she would request help. She placed these actions and people's names on the right side of the arrow corresponding to the activity that they would accomplish.

> *Building and maintaining*
> *mutually supportive relationships*
> *is essential if you are to*
> *successfully pursue a better life.*
> —STEDMAN GRAHAM

> *It takes a team*
> *to produce a winner.*
> —STEDMAN GRAHAM

Scan the QR Code below to purchase Stedman Graham's fabulous book, ***Identity: Your Passport to Success.***

Figure 6.5

Robin's Goal	
Activities that need to happen to achieve your goal	**Actions—who needs to do what to make this happen? By when?**
Apply to vet assistant schools and get accepted	• Put in my application • Get reference letters
Apply for financial aid/grant	• Get forms from school for grants/financial aid
Move into my new apartment	• Recruit family and friends with trucks to help me move
Check out local vet asst. schools	• Get on the internet to find local vet asst. schools • Call the schools and ask for info • Meet with the school staff for a fact finding meeting
Learn to use the computer better	• See what local adult education is available • Enroll in the adult ed class
Find an apartment	• Ask Cindy, Joe and Jacqueline to look for housing • Check the rental listings in the local paper
Get my previous school records	• Write to my high school and ask for my records
Stay in balance	• Meditate, journal, exercise and keep my plan alive!
Robin Now	

Step Five—Determine the Timeframe

Figure 6.6 depicts the due dates of the various actions required to achieve Robin's plan. Robin was aggressive with her timeframes but she knew that the school cycle in terms of financial aid and adult education actually worked with the time that she was building her plan with me. She also knew that she could get excellent references from people who knew what an intelligent, motivated person she was. Last, she knew that she might qualify for financial aid due to some personal circumstances. To find out what happens to Robin, see the next chapter where her plan was adjusted and measured over time.

Get the action habit—
you do not need to wait until
conditions are perfect.

—THE MAGIC OF
THINKING BIG

Figure 6.6

Robin's Goal	
Activities that need to happen to achieve your goal	**Actions— who needs to do what to make this happen? By when?**
Apply to vet assistant schools and get accepted	• Put in my application • Get reference letters **By 3/1**
Apply for financial aid/grant	• Get forms from school for grants/financial aid **By 3/1**
Move into my new apartment	• Recruit family and friends with trucks to help me move **By 1/15**
Check out local vet asst. schools	• Get on the internet to find local vet asst. schools • Call the schools and ask for info • Meet with the school staff for a fact finding meeting **By 1/15**
Learn to use the computer better	• See what local adult education is available **(by 12/15)** • Enroll in the adult ed class **By 12/15**
Find an apartment	• Ask Cindy, Joe and Jacqueline to look for housing • Check the rental listings in the local paper **By 12/1**
Get my previous school records	• Write to my high school and ask for my records **By 12/1**
Stay in balance	• Meditate, journal, exercise and keep my plan alive! **Ongoing**
Robin Now	

Working with homeless women

In 2003, I worked with homeless women on their life plans. Most of these women were extremely motivated to change their life situations. It was as if their backs were to the wall and they had to decide if they were going to come out swinging and survive or to sink into the wall, give up and die. For many of them their life plan was a matter of life or death.

I worked with Angie's Shelter, which is the women's portion of the New Horizons Homeless Shelter in Manchester, NH. I did eight life plans for eight of the homeless women. Angie's had a policy that nothing was to be put on the walls of the rooms. However, the exception was made for the life plans of the women. As we created the plans, the women wrote their plans in their own handwriting but I created a flip chart of each worksheet. A flip chart sheet was created for their talents and joys, their "I AM" statements, their missions in life, their dreams and their Life Choice Map. The women were allowed to hang these flip charts up on the walls. Many opted to have their dreams at the head of their beds and their life maps at the foot of their beds so that they could see them when they woke up. We gave each woman a set of metallic stars. The women mapped the progress of their plans with the stars so that each time they accomplished an action on their Life Choice Map, they gave themselves a star. Pretty soon, their maps were filled with stars! When we created the plan for each woman, I requested that the director of the women's program, Kathy Telge, also be a participant in the plan. This was extremely important because I did not know what programs were available locally and federally to help these women improve their lives. I requested that each woman work with Kathy weekly on the progress of her plan in order to get assistance if she needed it. I asked Kathy to keep me apprised of the women's progress. The last that I heard was within six months, five of the eight women had worked themselves out of being homeless! This was a huge success!

Two of the key ideas presented here are the importance of *need* and of *taking action*. In contrast, I have worked with other people who may or may not execute their plans. They want change but they are not motivated to make it happen on their behalf. They might complain a lot but they don't take the action to bring about the change that they are begging from God/the Universe.

The more active you are, the more energy you will have.

—THE POWER OF POSITIVE THINKING

How motivated are you?

In my career I have worked with over 11,000 people in 39 countries—some for life plans such as we are discussing in this book and others for business plans. The question always comes up on how best to ensure the success of a plan. One of the biggest factors to the success of *any* plan—be it a life plan or a business plan—is *how motivated are the plan creators to achieve the success of the plan?*

I once did a business plan for a group of business people in China. At the end of the plan I asked each team to stand up. I posed these questions to the team participants:

1. Do you think this plan is doable and achievable?
2. Do you believe that you can accomplish this plan?
3. Do you recommend that your Management team funds this plan?

One man stood up and asked through the translator, "Why does it matter what we believe? We are not the decision makers. We are not important." My answer was, "Are you the people who will execute this plan? If so, what you believe is of the *utmost importance* because what you think and what you believe is what you will actually accomplish. If you do not think that the plan is achievable, you won't make it. If you do not believe in the plan, you will not achieve it. The plan cannot succeed without your buy in." I then asked the man if this made sense to him and he and all of the other participants responded "Yes!"

> *One of the biggest factors to the success of*
> ANY *plan—be it a life plan or a business plan—*
> *is* how motivated are the plan creators
> to achieve the success of the plan?

In Chapter 3, I cited a quote from Napoleon Hill that says, "What the mind of man can conceive and believe, it can achieve." This statement ties our heads and our hearts together into belief. Without belief a plan will most likely fail. It's as if the subconscious mind sabotages the outcome. It's almost a foregone conclusion to the plan.

I have been asked many times why the plans for the homeless women were so successful. My answer comes down to necessity and belief. The first part of the answer is *desire*. These women had nowhere else to go—so most of them chose to fight back and succeed. They were motivated! The second part of the answer is *belief*. Some believed they could—*and they did!* Others believed they could not—*and they did not!*

> *Never be afraid to try something new. Remember, a lone amateur built the Ark.*
>
> *A large group of professionals built the Titanic.*
>
> —Dave Barry

Conversely, I have worked with many successful people who are not really motivated to make their plans work. They *say* that they want a change, but their beliefs and actions as they execute their plan reveal that they are complacent and are not motivated to make their plan a reality. So, the big question here is: *If YOU want to change YOUR LIFE, how motivated are YOU to turn YOUR PLAN into a reality?*

> *Be a busy person. People who are active are often much more at peace with themselves than those who are inactive and inert.*
>
> —The Sky's the Limit

Scan the QR Code below to download your *free* Sample Life Plan.

Key Points

Reminders:

Do	Don't
• Create a life choice map to determine how you can best get from *here* to *there* (your dream).	• Don't make impossible goals! Planning to be Pope may not work if you are not Catholic!
• Brainstorm all of the actions that you need to take—and all of the actions that you need others to take.	• Don't underestimate the power of creating a simple one page map. Just the act of drawing it out can consolidate your plan's strategy and execution details in your mind.
• Be realistic in the timeframes that you estimate. So many times, things may take longer than we expect.	
• Remember to take action! Also remember that taking 'no action' is taking the action of doing nothing. Sometimes doing nothing is appropriate to a plan and other times it is not. Do what you need to do to accomplish your dream! Don't get frustrated if your plan takes longer than you expected. Remember that Rome wasn't built in a day. Your dream might take longer to build than you expect—but stick with it and enjoy the ride!	

CHAPTER SEVEN

Measure and Adjust Your Life Plan

You can't control the wind,
but you can adjust your sails.

—Yiddish proverb

The importance of measurement

Congratulations! We've completely built a life plan. Now it's time to execute the plan, measure the results and adjust the plan if necessary. The questions you should be asking yourself are: "How exactly should I measure my plan? What is the best way to track the results of my plan? And, how should I adjust the plan if I need to?" Many people don't bother to measure their plans. They go along and continue to execute them but then they don't check back to see where they are. This seems to me like planning for the sake of planning—why do it to begin with? If you're going to create a plan, then make sure that it works!

Look at it this way. Let's say that you decided to take that drive from New York City to California that we spoke about in Chapter 5. Let's also say that you were on a tight schedule but you needed your car in Los Angeles, so you decided to drive. After Columbus, OH, much of the trip will be on Interstate 70 West. Let's say, though, that in St. Louis, MO, you got very tired and you missed your turn off onto Interstate 44 West. (This would be pretty easy to do because at that point the highway splits.) Now if you weren't paying attention to where you were (you weren't *measuring*), you could end up in a very different place than where you wanted to go initially. Taking this example to its extreme, Interstate 70 West ends at Interstate 15 in Utah. (You weren't supposed to go through Utah!) You could get back on track by taking Interstate 15 South to then get onto Interstate 40 West but this whole diversion would cost you a lot of time, miles and gas. It would have been much better to watch where you were to begin with and to measure your results in the first place!

How to measure and adjust your life plan

So exactly how do you measure your life plan? Simply put, you just see where you are against your plan. You make sure that the actions that needed to get done were, in fact, done.

Let's go into all of these points and use Robin's plan as an example. In the last chapter, Robin's Life Choice Map showed that she needed to accomplish certain activities by certain dates. Let's say that today's date is December 30th. By this point Robin should have:

- Written to her high school for her records. This was due on December 1st.
- Asked Cindy, Joe and Jacqueline to look for housing. This was due on December 1st.
- Checked the rental listings in the local paper. This was due on December 1st.
- Seen what local adult education was available. This was due on December 15th.
- Enrolled in the adult education class. This was due on December 15th.

> *How do you measure your life plan?*
> *Simply put, you just see where you are*
> *against your plan. You make sure that the actions*
> *that needed to get done were, in fact, done.*

Difficulties increase the nearer we approach the goal.

—JOHANN WOLFGANG
VON GOETHE

Figure 7.1

Robin's Goal	
Activities that need to happen to achieve your goal	**Actions— who needs to do what to make this happen? By when?**
Apply to vet assistant schools and get accepted	• Put in my application • Get reference letters **By 3/1**
Apply for financial aid/grant	• Get forms from school for grants/financial aid **By 3/1**
Move into my new apartment	• Recruit family and friends with trucks to help me move **By 1/15**
Check out local vet asst. schools	• Get on the internet to find local vet asst. schools • Call the schools and ask for info • Meet with the school staff for a fact finding meeting **By 1/15**
Learn to use the computer better	• See what local adult education is available **(by 12/15)** • Enroll in the adult ed class **By 12/15**
Find an apartment	• Ask Cindy, Joe and Jacqueline to look for housing • Check the rental listings in the local paper **By 12/1**
Get my previous school records	• Write to my high school and ask for my records **By 12/1**
Stay in balance	• Meditate, journal, exercise and keep my plan alive! **Ongoing**
Robin Now	

Figure 7.1 shows Robin's plan as it stood at the end of Chapter 6. To measure a plan, simply put a star near what has been done. Using Robin's map, we put stars on her accomplishments in Figure 7.2. Robin did indeed make a great deal of progress with her plan; she accomplished many of the actions that needed to be done. However, one very important action slipped in time: she was not able to get into the Computer Usage adult education course in the timeframe that she needed. The class was full. The mastery of this content was important for veterinary assistant school. If Robin had not found a way around this problem (Figure 7.3), she might not have been able to get into the veterinary assistant program because she would have missed a critical prerequisite.

Robin measured her plan. She watched what needed to be accomplished by what date. She knew that a vital milestone had been missed. She also knew that she was determined to accomplish her plan. She began to seek alternatives to the local adult education course. She discovered that she could actually take an online computer course and not only get the same content of information that she needed, but that she could get the prerequisite done faster because she was working at her own pace and was not dependent on a set class schedule. Robin successfully *adjusted* her life plan to meet her objectives, and she ultimately got the grant to go the veterinary assistant school!

When defeat comes, accept it as
a signal that your plans are not sound,
rebuild those plans, and set sail once more
toward your coveted goal.

—NAPOLEON HILL

Figure 7.2

Robin's Goal	
Activities that need to happen to achieve your goal	**Actions—who needs to do what to make this happen? By when?**
Apply to vet assistant schools and get accepted	• Put in application • Get reference letters **By 3/1**
Apply for financial aid/grant	• Get forms from school for grants/financial aid **By 3/1**
Move into my new apartment	• Recruit family and friends with trucks to help me move **By 1/15**
Check out local vet asst. schools	• Get on the internet to find local vet asst. schools • Call the schools and ask for info • Meet with the school staff for a fact finding meeting **By 1/15**
Learn to use the computer better	✪ See what local adult education is available **(by 12/15)**
	• Enroll in the adult ed class **By 12/15**
Find an apartment	✪ Ask Cindy, Joe and Jacqueline to look for housing ✪ Check the rental listings in the local paper
	By 12/1
Get my previous school records	✪ Write to my high school and ask for my records
	By 12/1
Stay in balance	✪ Meditate, journal, exercise and keep my plan alive!
	Ongoing
Robin Now	

139

So how do you adjust your life plan? If you miss an important milestone, you brainstorm (alone or with others) what other things can be done to make up for this missed milestone. Ask yourself, "How can I achieve my objective in a different way?" Sometimes this might mean that a completely different set of actions needs to take place from the ones that you started your plan with. However, if you don't measure, you might not even realize that you missed an important milestone!

If you find a goal has changed for you,
be sure to acknowledge that to yourself.
Get clear in your mind the fact that
you are no longer focusing on your previous goal.
End the cycle of the old, and begin the cycle
of the new. This helps you avoid getting confused,
or feeling that you've "failed" when you
have simply changed.

—SHAKTI GAWAIN,
CREATIVE VISUALIZATION

Figure 7.3

Robin's Goal	
Activities that need to happen to achieve your goal	Actions— who needs to do what to make this happen? By when?
Apply to vet assistant schools and get accepted	• Put in application • Get reference letters **By 3/1**
Apply for financial aid/grant	• Get forms from school for grants/financial aid **By 3/1**
Move into my new apartment	• Recruit family and friends with trucks to help me move **By 1/15**
Check out local vet asst. schools	• Get on the internet to find local vet asst. schools • Call the schools and ask for info • Meet with the school staff for a fact finding meeting **By 1/15**
Learn to use the computer better	♦ Take an online computer course and complete it by 1/15 **By 1/15**
Find an apartment	✪ Ask Cindy, Joe and Jacqueline to look for housing ✪ Check the rental listings in the local paper **By 12/1**
Get my previous school records	✪ Write to my high school and ask for my records **By 12/1**
Stay in balance	✪ Meditate, journal, exercise and keep my plan alive! **Ongoing**
Robin Now	

*When you achieve a goal, be sure to acknowledge
consciously to yourself that it has been completed.
Often we achieve things that we have been
desiring and visualizing, and we forget to even
notice that we have succeeded!
So give yourself some appreciation and a pat
on the back, and be sure to thank the universe
for fulfilling your requests.*

—Shakti Gawain,
Creative Visualization

*How do you adjust your life plan?
If you miss an important milestone, you brainstorm
(alone or with others) what other things can be done
to make up for this missed milestone. Ask yourself,
"How can I achieve my objective in a different way?"
Get around the obstacle if you can't go through it!*

Key Points

Reminders:

Do	Don't
■ Keep track of what is happening in your life. Measure and adjust your life plan!	■ Do not put your life plan in a desk drawer or on a shelf! Your life should NOT be collecting dust! It's much more important than that!
■ Place the activities that you need to keep yourself in balance on your Life Choice Map and adjust them as needed.	■ Don't forget to congratulate yourself for achieving your whole goal or even pieces of your goal. Remember that moving forward is movement! Sometimes we need to move slowly to build up the speed necessary to overcome inertia!
■ Remember, change is a part of life. Adjust your plan as needed.	
■ Stay in tune with the Higher You. Stay in balance! This is important for your ongoing health!	■ Don't give up! If you miss an important milestone, brainstorm what other things can be done to make up for this missed milestone. Ask yourself, "How can I achieve my objective in a different way?" Stick with your plan and adjust it as need be!
■ When you complete an activity, a milestone or a goal, be sure to give yourself a "well done" and a pat on the back! You deserve to have your accomplishments acknowledged. Feel free to tell those who love you what you've achieved. Share your success with others. It can motivate them as much as it motivates you!	

Harmonic Alignment—Closing the Loop with Balance

Anybody can succeed—if they make a plan,
and keep taking whatever steps they can
toward the fulfillment of that plan.

—MARC ALLEN

What is *harmonic alignment*? The best definition that I have seen came from a blogsite on the Internet called "Mickie's Zoo." In one of the blogs, Mickie says,

> *Harmonic Alignment is a state where the body, mind and spirit are in an optimized energetic state. When we are in this harmonized state there is an instant increase in strength, flexibility, endurance, coordination and balance. There is also a reduction in stress and anxiety, improved learning, focus, intuition, creativity and concentration.*

Although this definition of Harmonic Alignment was given in reference to music, the definition is very apropos to what this book is all about.

In the last chapter we created a Life Choice Map. As you move forward with your plan, it is important to see where you are and to adjust the plan as *life happens.* Keep moving forward! Keep taking the steps needed to get *there* from *here*—wherever *here* and *there* are now! As you move forward, remember that it is really important to stay in balance. We, as human beings, are happiest when we are in balance.

So now let's close the loop and finalize the plan—and in doing so, we started with and we'll end with balance!

Of all the people in the world,
how many of them dare to dream
their greatest dreams?
And of those who do,
how many actually sit down
and make a plan in writing
to reach those dreams?
And how many of them take action,
and keep taking the steps
they need to take?

—MARC ALLEN

How to use the other quadrants to bring yourself back into balance

In Chapter 1 we discussed the four components of balance: Intellectual, Physical, Emotional, and Spiritual. As you execute your plan, continue to focus on your own balance. There are counterbalance techniques that you can use to align yourself into a better balanced state. Sometimes people use one component where they are strong to counterbalance another component where they are weak. They employ a strategy of overcompensating in one area to balance out a deficiency in another area.

Let me be more specific. Did you ever notice that when some people are emotionally upset they go for a run or they do some other physical activity to deal with their emotional distress? They release their emotional stress through physically working out their bodies. By doing this, they are using their bodies to bring their feelings and their emotions back into balance. Figure 8.1 depicts that the Emotional is being "pulled" by the Physical.

Figure 8.1

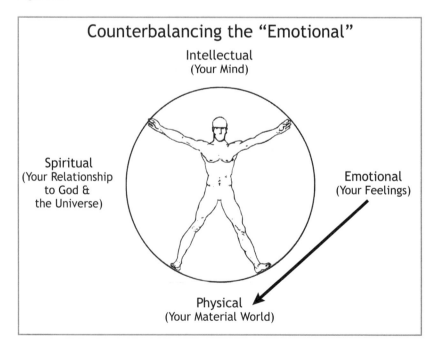

Counterbalancing the "Emotional"

Intellectual
(Your Mind)

Spiritual
(Your Relationship
to God &
the Universe)

Emotional
(Your Feelings)

Physical
(Your Material World)

Did you ever see the movie, "A Beautiful Mind"? If so, you will remember that the main character, John Forbes Nash Jr., was suffering from schizophrenia, which is a disease of the brain. It is a physical disorder. John saw and spoke with people who didn't exist, people who were figments of his imagination. In order to bring himself back into balance, he counterbalanced himself by using his mind (his intellect) and his love for his wife (his emotions) to pull himself back into balance and overcome his disease. It wasn't always easy but he employed this strategy to stay in balance. See Figure 8.2.

Figure 8.2

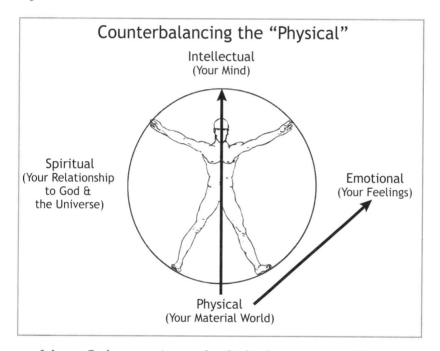

Johnny Cash was a singer who died a few years ago. There was a lot of television coverage of his life after his death. One documentary showed him in an interview in the late 1980s. During the interview, Johnny discussed his addiction to amphetamines and tranquilizers. In the 1960s, his addiction was at its peak; he needed "uppers" to wake up and "downers" to fall asleep. He was a bag of bones and was at the point of death. June Carter and her family intervened with him and June begged him to go for help, which he did. Johnny Cash admitted to himself that he was an addict and would be one the rest of his life. He used his mind (Intellectual), his love for June Carter (Emotional) and his strong belief in God (Spiritual) to fight his addiction (Physical) every day of his life. See Figure 8.3.

Figure 8.3

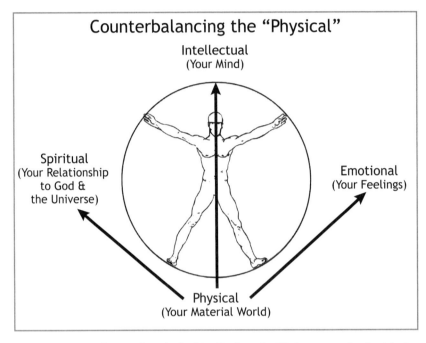

Counterbalancing the "Physical"

Intellectual
(Your Mind)

Spiritual
(Your Relationship
to God &
the Universe)

Emotional
(Your Feelings)

Physical
(Your Material World)

Many people use their belief in God or the Universe to deal with the problems that they face in life. They might use their minds (their will) and their belief in God to overcome problems from any other area such as a physical disease, emotional problems, financial problems, mental problems or intellectual challenges. My friend, Lionel, is an alcoholic. He uses the Physical to counterbalance the Physical—his body to counterbalance his body. Let me be more specific. Lionel has used physical activities such as running and competitive skiing combined with his Spiritual aspect (his belief in God, meditation and prayer) to "pull" his alcohol addiction back into balance for the past twenty years. This approach works for him and as he has said many times, if he didn't do it, he could go back to drinking in a heartbeat. See Figure 8.4.

Figure 8.4

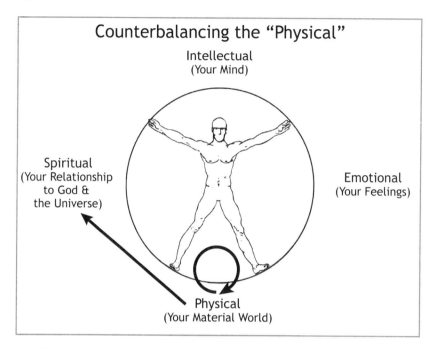

It is common for people in our society to believe that the mind is the most important aspect of the body. Too many people overuse their minds so that their minds are constantly in full gear. They never release their minds or let their minds rest. It is as if their minds are gerbils on a wheel that never stops. They have overactive minds which they need to calm down. As with the other counterbalancing approaches, you can use your body, your emotions or communication with God/the Universe to help you to calm your mind down. Just as running or other physical activities help to counterbalance emotions, they also help to counterbalance the mind. As meditation and prayer helps to counterbalance the Emotional and the Physical, it also helps to counterbalance the Intellectual. See Figure 8.5.

Emotion can also be used to counterbalance the Intellectual. I have seen so many people who were workaholics, who used their minds nonstop, fall in love and finally find balance in their lives. By the way, it is commonly observed by psychiatrists that someone with Obsessive Compulsive Disorder (OCD)—which in my model affects the Intellectual and the Physical—can become "cured" when they fall in love. See Figure 8.5.

Figure 8.5

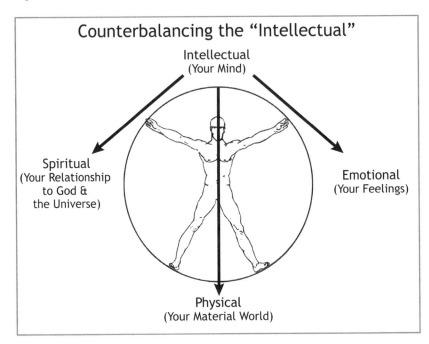

Lastly, let's talk about how many people cope with their world when it is falling apart at its seams. I did a life plan for Louis, who is 34 years old and has a young family. He was getting a lot of pressure from his work and as a result was under a lot of stress. His mind became overactive as he thought about ways to improve his performance on his job. Louis found himself becoming more and more anxious and depressed—and the more anxious and depressed he became, the more tired his body became. Because Louis had a young family, his wife couldn't work as much as they wanted. They both agreed that she should work part time from the house. This, however, put them under increased financial pressure.

If we look at Louis' life, he was out of balance with his Intellectual (his mind was overactive), Physical (he had financial problems and he was constantly tired) and Emotional (he often felt anxious and depressed) aspects. When we did his life plan, Louis came to the conclusion that he needed to use his Spirit (Spiritual) to counterbalance everything else. He began to meditate every morning and every night, and as he meditated, he turned inward and found God. Little by little, Louis' life began to shift. The more he meditated the better he was able to calm his mind and his fears. He realized that his anxiety was affecting his performance on the job. He also realized that this job was not the best place to put his talents. Louis asked to be transferred to a different role and by doing this, things not only improved for him tremendously on the job but they also improved for him in his home life. This transition took several months, but over time, Louis' balance was restored. So, in Louis' case, he used the Spiritual aspect of his life to bring the Intellectual, the Physical and the Emotional aspects of his life back into balance. See Figure 8.6.

Figure 8.6

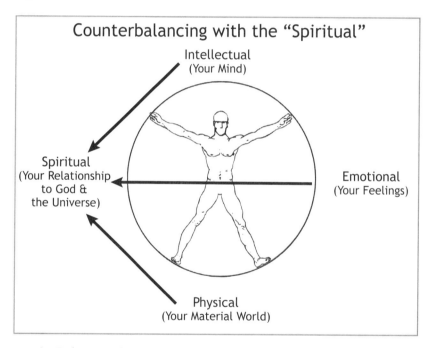

As I discussed these thoughts with a woman named JoAnn for whom I did a life plan, she said, "I always go for a run up the side of a mountain when I'm stressed. Actually it relieves the pressure of my day but I never knew what I was subconsciously doing!" Think about counterbalancing strategies for yourself. I would bet that you already employ them, though you might not be conscious of doing so. Now that you know how to use them, consciously decide how to bring yourself back into balance by counter-balancing with the other quadrant points.

How to speed up your plan

In the last chapter, we looked at a Life Choice Map of a young woman named Robin, who wanted to become a veterinary assistant. In Robin's plan, you can see that by changing an activity, Robin actually accomplished one of her objectives faster than she had originally planned. She did not do this on purpose, but that was the end result. When you are doing your life plan and you map out your activities, you might find that the total timeframe does not meet your needs. This might be because one of the steps is taking too long—or all of them just take too long. This is when you need to be creative. You need to "think outside of the box." Brainstorm ideas on how to achieve the objective *faster*. Share your plan with others and create a Mastermind group!

Share your plan with people who support and believe in you

Sometimes it's difficult to execute your life plan by yourself. You might need physical help and support from others as well as moral support. I recommend that you share your plan with positive people—with people who will support you both morally and with physical actions if required. I also recommend that you avoid sharing your plan with people who might put you down or with those who tell you that you "can't." These people might suck the life out of your plan; they might defeat it and you before you even begin.

Establish a Mastermind Alliance

- *A mastermind alliance consists of two or more minds working actively together in perfect harmony toward a common definite objective.*
- *Through a mastermind alliance you can appropriate and use the full strength of the experience, training, and knowledge of others just as if they were your own.*
- *No individual has ever achieved success without the help and cooperation of others.*
- *The value of "gathering together those of a like mind" is self-evident.*
- *A group of brains coordinated in a spirit of harmony will provide more thought energy than a single brain, just as a group of electric batteries will provide more energy than a single battery.*

—Napoleon Hill

Share your plan with those who love you and those who believe in you. You can call these people your "Mastermind" group. Their task is to brainstorm about your plan with you and to help you achieve it as quickly and efficiently as possible. They can come up with successful ideas that you hadn't even considered! You don't need to work with them all at once; you can talk to them one at a time and get their ideas. I employ this technique in many ways in my life. I have different Master-mind groups for different things that I want to achieve and I love being in another person's Mastermind group. It is my way of *paying back* and also *paying forward* for the assistance that I have received from so many others.

Whatever you do, don't give up!

As I've mentioned before, I've worked with thousands of people in creating both life plans and business plans. One thing I can tell you for certain: plans will not always go as you planned! From the plans I've seen and the many people that I've worked with, several things mark the difference between success and failure.

They are:

- The willingness to observe what is happening
- The willingness to take action and adjust the plan as needed
- The willingness and stamina to not lose faith in yourself and in God/the Universe if things go wrong
- A "never say die" attitude.

I once attended a sales training course where the instructor was speaking about setbacks. We were talking about cold calling, which is when people call other people who they do not know to talk business opportunities with them on the phone or in person. Many cold calls result in rejection. (You've probably received these calls from telemarketers more times than you want!) What the sales trainer said was,

> Try to think of these calls not as personal rejections but as people simply saying "no." If you are a waitperson in a restaurant and you ask someone if they want another cup of coffee and they reply "no," you do not lose your self-esteem or take it personally. Sometimes people just say "no" because whatever you are suggesting does not work for them at that point in time.

Nothing in the world can take the place of persistence. Talent will not; nothing is more common than unsuccessful men with talent. Genius will not; unrewarded genius is almost a proverb. Education will not; the world is full of educated derelicts. Persistence and determination alone are omnipotent.

—CALVIN COOLIDGE

My purpose in telling you this is that we all face setbacks at one time or another. Things don't *always* go as planned. When this happens, it is important for us to move forward with our plans. I know that it sometimes is discouraging to receive a lot of "no"s when you really want and need someone else to say "yes," but this is the time when it is most important for you to go inside of yourself to find out if what you are trying to do is correct for you and your life.

I once lived on the upper West side of Manhattan when I was in my 20s. There was a local newspaper that ran an ad to buy the following quote which was printed up in a small poster:

> *Our mission is to analyze the situation and, through foresight and advanced planning, avoid or circumvent problems before they arise. Should the unexpected occur, then our aim is to swiftly and efficiently arrive at a workable solution... however, when you're up to your ass in alligators, it's difficult to remember that your initial objective was to drain the swamp.*

I have never been able to find out who wrote this complete quote. I've found bits and pieces of it on many Internet sites. The quote, though, really gets to the point that I've been trying to make. We are doing the best that we can in creating our life plans. We're trying to anticipate all of the potential problems and put together a plan that not only accounts for all of them, but a plan that achieves the objectives that we want as quickly and efficiently as possible. Sometimes, however, things don't go our way, and then the "alligators" show up. Remember, when this happens, don't lose sight of your objective! Stick with your plan!

Sometimes it is more important to discover what one cannot do, than what one can do.

—LIN YUTANG

Please refer back to Todd's Life Plan Drawing in Chapter 4. Todd said, "Mary, during the difficult past few years, I pulled out my Life Plan drawing many times to keep me grounded in what matters most to me." Please remember this and learn from it. When things don't go as you planned, go back to your drawing and remember your dreams! Go back to your plan and rework your Life Choice Map! Go back to your plan, regroup, take action, measure and adjust until you meet your objectives or until you decide that you want something else.

How do we know what we're supposed to do?

People always ask me, "How do I know what I'm supposed to do? I know that I'm supposed to do *something*—I'm here on this earth for a reason—but I just don't know what that *something* is." To this I reply, "Go inward." Look for the answer inside of you. It's in *here*—not out *there*. By this I mean that in order to really know who you are and what is really important to you, you need to ask this of the Higher You. The best way to do this is through meditation and prayer.

Let's say, though, that through prayer and meditation, you've determined that you need to achieve a certain goal. You know where you ultimately want to go but when you analyze your life choices, you find out that there are many ways for you to achieve this goal and that one is not more significantly better than another. Now you're confused. You're not sure whether you're supposed to do *this* or *that*.

When people come to this point, this is what I suggest: do a lot of targeted activities. Put a lot "out there" but make sure that they fit with your plan. Then see what works. I sometimes say to my clients, "Throw a whole bunch of cooked spaghetti at the wall and see what sticks!"

Sometimes, though, it feels as if nothing sticks. We get frustrated and angry that it is taking so long to achieve our plan. It is times like these when I remind my clients and myself of what my mother (who is a very wise woman) used to tell me: "When the door closes, God will open a window. When you can't find an open window, look for a vent. *Something* will open up. Be patient. It *will* happen."

How to keep in balance as you execute your plan

It is so easy to lose balance in life—particularly as we try to achieve a certain goal. Many of us tend to frantically move from action to action in executing our plans. The life planning process that I've shared with you is intended to be a *closed loop* system. What this means is that it's important for you to continue to check back with your plan—not to stick it on a shelf or in a drawer to collect dust. After all, it's *your* life plan, so keep it alive—as your life is alive.

As you execute your plan, go back to the activities that you decided upon in Chapter 1 to stay in balance. Make sure that you've entered these activities into your plan. If you don't stay in balance it will be harder for you to achieve your plan. Did you ever read *Alice's Adventures in Wonderland*? Do you remember when Alice is running in a circle with the Red Queen? Alice is running as fast as she can but is not going anywhere, and the Red Queen says, "Now! Now! ... Faster! Faster!" That's what it's like to execute your plan and run from activity to activity. You run in a circle, you get exhausted, and you wonder if you are making any progress at all. I call this the "Alice in Wonderland and the Red Queen Syndrome." Many people just run, run, run. They do activity after activity and they do not measure their plans nor do they stay in balance. If they would just measure their plans, they might find that when they are running in a circle, it might be tempting to change their *speed* and run faster, but actually what is really needed is for them to change their *direction*. This would be a lot more obvious to them if they took the time to measure their results!

The four magic words—"Say, Do, Measure, Adjust!"

In this methodology, there are four magic words that sum up the key things for you to remember. They are *Say, Do, Measure, Adjust!*

- *Say:* What you say is "true" about yourself is *true* in your mind. What you say "will happen" mostly likely *will occur*. It will happen as *you say*! This is a factor of your belief about yourself.
- *Do:* What you do will get results. Keep going. Chip away at it; you'll get results sooner or later!
- *Measure:* Measure and watch your plan. See what has happened and measure where you are.
- *Adjust:* Adjust your actions and your plan if you need to. Keep your eye on maintaining your balance and on achieving your goals.

Remember the wise words of Kahlil Gibran: "In every winter's heart, there is a quivering spring and behind the veil of each night, there is a smiling dawn." It might feel like winter to you today but spring is right around the corner. Don't lose faith and hope! You'll succeed if you stick to your plan and take action! Remember, *Say, Do, Measure, Adjust!*

What's next after I achieve my plan?

Many times, people have put together great plans and then once they set out to achieve them, changes have occurred in their lives or new opportunities have presented themselves. These events have required them to adjust their life plans.

I'd like to refer back to Caroline's Life Plan drawing in Chapter 4. Caroline is a very talented individual. To be more explicit about Caroline's life plan, when she and I created it, we followed all of the steps in Chapter 5. We created six Ben Franklin 'T' charts for her. We then took these six options and created a Life Choices Assessment Tool. Choice number six seemed like the best option for her, so we created that plan and she began to execute it. However, life is strange. As Caroline set out to execute the plan for choice number six, a seventh choice came to her attention. Because she learned how to use the Ben Franklin 'T' chart method and the Life Choices Assessment Tool, she was able to map out this seventh choice on her own. It won hands down; it was by far the best option for her. Today, Caroline has completed this part of her life plan. She is now ready to move on to a new life plan—one that will have a whole new set of dreams—because as she grows, so do her dreams!

After all, life *really* doesn't end. Life changes—and change is inevitable (as are death and taxes)! We might not always like change and we might not always embrace it, but life is much smoother, and in the long run, happier for us once we accept it. As part of our lives and the changes in our lives, we dream our dreams and they change too.

When you're finished changing, you're finished.

—BENJAMIN FRANKLIN

As healthy human beings, we are *always* dreaming the next dream—and, even if we don't know that we are doing it consciously, we are doing it subconsciously. This is part of growing, changing and maturing.

So, as I leave you to dream *your* dreams and to create *your* life plans, remember that it is healthy to embrace and enjoy life—*YOUR* LIFE!

Life is change. Growth is optional. Choose wisely.

—WALT DISNEY

IT'S *YOUR* LIFE—WHAT DO *YOU* WANT TO DO WITH IT?

(Remember Always: *Dream … Achieve … Dream some more … Achieve some more … and Enjoy the ride!*)

Key Points

Reminders:

Do	Don't
<ul><li>Employ a "counterbalance" strategy to compensate for areas where you are weak or out of balance.</li><li>You will succeed if you stick to your plan and take action!</li><li>Remember my mother's admonition, "When the door closes, God will open a window. When you can't find an open window, look for a vent. *Something* will open up. Be patient. It *will* happen."</li><li>Remember the four Magic Words: *Say, Do, Measure, Adjust!*</li><li>Remember always: *Dream … Achieve … Dream some more … Achieve some more … and Enjoy the ride!*</li></ul>	<ul><li>Don't *ever* give up on yourself! You are here in this world for a reason! Go deep within yourself and dream your dreams into reality! Stick with your plan! Persist and persevere! You are worth it!</li><li>Think twice about sharing your plan with negative people who might defeat it and you before you even begin. I encourage you to share your plan with people who love you and who believe in you.</li><li>Avoid the "Alice in Wonderland and the Red Queen Syndrome." Measure your plan and focus on your balance. Instead of *changing your speed and running faster*, you might be best served to *change your direction!*</li></ul>

Start designing your own destiny with Mary's 6 week Life Planning Session. Scan the QR Code below and get started today!

Epilogue

As I mentioned previously, in 2003, I was asked to speak with a group of 25 homeless women in Manchester, NH. As I prepared to meet with these women, I thought to myself, "What can I possibly say to these women? Their backs are against the wall. Many of them have 'seen it all.' How can I help them? What can I say to them that will make a difference in their lives?" I realized that the best thing that I could do for them was to create a tool—a process—that would help them get from *here* to *there* (wherever they wanted *there* to be).

When I went in to speak with the women, I brought a flip chart stand and markers with me. I gave each of them the first two pictures that you see in Chapter 1—the "How in Balance Are You?" and the "Balance Scorecard" pictures. I also gave each of them the "What Do You Need to Get Back into Balance?" worksheet. We talked for over two hours. Everyone was talking to me and to each other. The director of the shelter, Kathy Telge, was amazed because some of these women were drunk, drugged or they just wouldn't talk to anyone. Yet, we all talked about life experiences and how to get back into balance.

At the end of the time together I offered to do a life plan for four women—that they could "raffle me off" when I left and I'd do a two hour in-depth plan for each of the winners. I told them that because I didn't know much about what services were available to them, I would need to have Kathy in on the planning sessions so that she could help to create the plan with us.

As was mentioned previously, I ultimately did eight plans for these women. The primary concepts used in this book are the original concepts that I presented to them. I gave each woman a binder with a set of planning materials, markers, pens, pencils, paper for drawing and the sticky stars mentioned in Chapter 6. Many of the materials given to the women are similar but not as in-depth to what you see in this book today. (Many of the tools have been modified and enhanced throughout the years.)

After several months, I was able to track these women through Kathy. I learned that five of the eight women were no longer homeless.

One woman got a job in a local VA Hospital where she convinced the staff to train her to maintain medical equipment. Another sold her knitted personalized children's wear in an upscale boutique. Still another woman got a job driving a shuttle bus for a local hotel to/from the airport. She also cooked the snacks for the hotel guests. Kathy told me recently that she ran into one of the women just last year. The woman was working at a gas station, got an apartment and got her children back from Child Services. The woman told Kathy how much better her life had become.

Although I lost track of these women over time, I will be forever grateful to them for starting me on a whole new journey in my life—working with people to create, execute, measure and adjust their life plans aimed at making their dreams come true!

I hope this book has helped you too!

May you *always* live the life of your dreams!

Start designing your own destiny with an exclusive one-on-one Life Planning Session! Scan the QR Code below and get started today!

About the Author—Mary A. Molloy

Mary Molloy has over 35 years of experience in Sales, Sales Management, Marketing Management, International Marketing, Business and Life Coaching and the Training of Sales and Marketing Professionals. Mary coauthored *The Buck Starts Here—Profit Based Sales and Marketing Made Easy*, which is currently available in most major bookstores. *The Buck Starts Here* won the Clarion Award for the best nonfiction book of the year.

Mary began her career in 1974 as a Junior High, High School and College Math Teacher. In 1976, Mary joined IBM and became the first woman to successfully sell computers for IBM in the New York Garment District. After leaving IBM, Mary ran two successful Software Companies and then, in, 1984, joined Digital Equipment Corporation to run S.E.L.L. (Digital's premiere Sales School) and to train Digital's Sales force in business and financial selling. Mary received Digital's Instructor Excellence Award in 1986 and was named "Woman of the Year" by the New Hampshire YWCA in 1987. Mary held several senior Marketing positions within Digital, one of which was to run 25% of DECworld '90 which was Digital's most important trade show. In this capacity, Mary led a 1,100 person team to provide content and demonstrations of Digital's Information Systems Solutions to 40,000 customers. For this work, Mary received Digital's 1990 Marketing Leadership Award.

In 1990, Mary created TRB Consulting Group with her partner, Michael Molloy. TRB Consulting Group has worked with over 16,000 Sales, Marketing and Business professionals in 39 countries, from very large corporations to very small companies. Mary personally has worked with 11,000 of these professionals. TRB's clients include HP/Compaq Computer Corporation, Microsoft, Motorola, Siemens Healthcare, Invensys Corporation and hundreds of other small-to-medium sized companies worldwide who want to drive Profit-based, Profit-driven Sales and Marketing organizations.

After Mary coauthored *The Buck Starts Here*, she started to write another business book called *Sales Messages That Sell*. That all changed one night when Mary had a dream to write a different book. The dream said to write a book called *The Partnering Ten Commandments—Partner for Profit* where she actually dreamt the ten commandment chapter titles. (*The Partnering Ten Commandments* is a business book on how companies can partner effectively and will be published in the near future.)

In 2003, Mary took her business planning methodology to a whole new level. She added spirituality and metaphysics to it in order to create an entire life planning methodology. The feedback from professionals in the coaching and counseling field is that the *Design Your Own Destiny — Life Planning for the 21st Century* methodology is unlike any they've seen in life planning. It is unique because it focuses on each person as a whole; it focuses on their Minds, their Material world (their Health and their Wealth), their Relationship with God or the Universe and their Emotions. By incorporating the best practices of a great business planning methodology with spirituality and metaphysics, Mary has created a process that enables people of all ages worldwide to create a life plan that will achieve their dreams!

Acknowledgements

- To my husband, Paul Brown, thank you for *always* being there for me. You encouraged me to finish this book—and you proofread and edited every word. You are such a love and a true friend.

- To my mother, Mary Gagliardo, who has been my biggest cheerleader since I was born! Mom, you were my first spiritual mentor. You have unbelievable strength, great wisdom and incredible faith—and boy, are you "tuned in"!

- To Beatrice Napolitano, my second mother. You've got the greatest attitude and strength. Thank you for years of love and encouragement.

- To my daughter, Jennifer Payson. Jen, you've been with me through thick and thin. You have an incredibly powerful mind, great drive and excellent marketing sense. You are such an incredibly wonderful daughter! Thank you for all of your help through the years.

- To Kelsey, my gorgeous granddaughter. You can't read this yet— but one day you will! Kelsey, Gigi thanks God for you! You came into my life right when I needed you! You are a true gift!

- To Judi Brown for the fabulous job of editing my first version of this book. Thanks for your enthusiasm and encouragement— as well as to Virginia Virgil, Sonia Javier Obinger, Deborah Slobodnik, Don Herbener and Laura Rivela for proofreading with excellent comments/feedback.

- To Dr. Harold Silverman, author of *The Pill Book* for his outstanding and much appreciated assistance in determining how to best publish this book.

- To Kellie Thinnes Hamel for being my spiritual mentor. Your views on life, love, friendship and Spirit have been a true inspiration.

- To my four Deborahs: Deborah Seter, Deborah Svenson, Deborah Cannon and Deborah Slobodnik. You guys have been there for me—each of you in your own powerful way. Thank you for being the gifts that you are!

- To Pete Markwith. You were the first person to brainstorm this book with me. Your guidance, thoughts, impressions and ideas helped me to shape my own thoughts about God and the Universe. (And thank you so much for turning me on to Ernest Holmes!)

- To the Gagliardo and Pellicane families. My brothers, Michael and John. My sister, Nancy. My nephew, Joseph. My brother in law, Tim Donofrio. My aunt, Jean. My cousins, Mary, Neal and Michael. And all of my other cousins and aunts and uncles. I can't list you all for sheer space reasons but you've all been "there" for me through all of the ups and downs of life. When Michael died, you encouraged me. When things went wrong, you consoled me. When things went right, you cheered for me. Thank you! What more can I say?

- To Elisabeth, Jordan and Michael Brown for being great kids, as well as to the rest of the Brown family for being so supportive.

- To Michael Molloy, Christine Molloy, Matt Arnold, Jack Arnold, Lucas Molloy, Billy Molloy, PJ Molloy, Barbara Molloy, Claudia Wysocki and Dan Wysocki and the rest of the Molloy Clan for being such important parts of my life for over 35 years.

- To Lenny Emery, Ginny Virgil (my book buddy!), Joann Vollmer, Linda Richards, Thankam Rangala, Ray Thorpe and Elizabeth Rix. Each of you plays such a huge part in my life. Thank you for sharing your thoughts, spiritual insights and journeys with me.

- To Carol Melis, Barbara Annis, Kevin Glynn, Joan Jacobs, Cathy Shea, Kathleen Moore, Dianne Durkin—do you believe how far back we go and we still love, help and support each other?

- To the town of Waterville Valley and its residents. You have all been there for me for so many years. I am so grateful to live in such a wonderful place surrounded by such incredible people! Thank you for everything!

- To my Waterville buddies—Marilyn Clarkson, Barbara Stout, Nancy Grimes, Luda Caefer and Lynne Nesbitt. I love you guys!

- To my Peru brothers and sisters led by Pierre Garreault, Vilma Pinedo and the other Peruvian masters. Kim Doucette, Michael & Kellie Hamel, Christine Kuhlman, Marcy Blass, Liz Henderson Dave Hendrixson and Veronique & Jean Paul Crouzoulon—we went through so much together. Thank you for helping to heal me.

- To Michael Morin and JoAnne Cordero—the best technical people who I have ever had the pleasure to work with! Michael, you are so loved and so missed!

- To Liz McNeill Jenkins for all of the love, friendship, help and support through the years—not to mention your *incredibly* talented photographs!!

- To Susan Kimper, Alyssa Herb and Terry Kimper for your help in adjusting the methodology to the nursing profession
- To Tom Gross for helping me to brainstorm book titles on such short notice!
- To Kathy Telge and the women of Angie's Shelter for starting this journey with me. Thank you!
- To all of the people who took the survey to determine the best title and book jacket cover for this book—thank you! You made such a difference!
- To Stephen Hodecker for drawing a perfect "balance figure"!
- To Diane Angelucci for initially editing my book and to Dina of FirstEditing.com for the final edit.
- The the DYOD Launch team—Carol White, Anita Jones, Bob Smith, Jacqueline C. Simonds, Jennifer Molloy Payson, Kristin Andress, Josh P. Wills, Mahijeet Singh, Rob Nissen and Cathy Paper—I never could have done it without you! You are all amazing and have gone the extra mile! Thank you!
- To Marc Allen for helping out a total stranger with so much energy, feedback and targeted advice. Marc, you have impacted me and so many others. Thank you!
- To Stedman Graham for your belief in me and my work. Your "out of the box" strategic thinking, insight and wisdom have provided me so much encouragement, direction and focus. Stedman, you have made such a big difference! Thank you for everything!

Index